TWAYNE'S WORLD AUTHORS SERIES

A Survey of the World's Literature

Sylvia Bowman, Indiana University
GENERAL EDITOR

GERMANY

Ulrich Weisstein, Indiana University
EDITOR

Grimmelshausen

(TWAS 291)

TWAYNE'S WORLD AUTHORS SERIES (TWAS)

The purpose of TWAS is to survey the major writers
—novelists, dramatists, historians, poets, philosophers,
and critics—of the nations of the world. Among the
national literatures covered are those of Australia,
Canada, China, Eastern Europe, France, Germany,
Greece, India, Italy, Japan, Latin America, the Neth-
erlands, New Zealand, Poland, Russia, Scandinavia,
Spain, and the African nations, as well as Hebrew,
Yiddish, and Latin Classical literatures. This survey
is complemented by Twayne's United States Authors
Series and English Authors Series.

The intent of each volume in these series is to present
a critical-analytical study of the works of the writer;
to include biographical and historical material that
may be necessary for understanding, appreciation,
and critical appraisal of the writer; and to present all
material in clear, concise English—but not to vitiate
the scholarly content of the work by doing so.

Grimmelshausen

By KENNETH NEGUS

Rutgers University

Twayne Publishers, Inc.   ::   New York

Library of Congress Cataloging in Publication Data
Negus, Kenneth.
    Grimmelshausen.
    (Twayne's world authors series, TWAS 291. Germany)
    Bibliography: p.
    1. Grimmelshausen, Hans Jacob Christoffel von,
1625–1676.
PT1732.N4   1974   833'.5   73–17215
ISBN 0–8057–2405–2

MANUFACTURED IN THE UNITED STATES OF AMERICA

For Niki, Chris, and Jon

Preface

The purpose of this book is to introduce both the general reader and the scholar of German literature to all important aspects of Grimmelshausen's life and works. It is the first book of this description written in English, and only the second in any language. Preceding mine is Günther Weydt's valuable little handbook (in the Metzler series), *Hans Jacob Christoffel von Grimmelshausen,* which appeared in 1971. Most of my book had been written before his was available to me. By means of brief latter-stage revisions and notes I have, however, taken into account many views and items of information appearing in Weydt's book.

The emphasis of this monograph—in contrast to Weydt's survey— is less on textual criticism, literary sources, and bibliography, and more on the literary qualities and relative artistic merits of Grimmelshausen's prose works. My ultimate aim was to offer the reader an overview and total evaluation of his accomplishments as a writer. This seems to be a timely task, for thanks to Weydt and his predecessors (Bechtold, Könnecke, Scholte, and Koschlig), most of the textual and documentary groundwork that was still feasible in our century has probably been accomplished—barring the remote possibility of major additional discoveries in archives and libraries. And a complete scholarly edition of Grimmelshausen's works is now appearing under the careful editorship of Rolf Tarot, assisted by Wolfgang Bender and Franz Günter Sieveke.

There are still serious and frustrating gaps in our knowledge of Grimmelshausen. His year of birth remains uncertain; important milestones in his life (such as the date of his conversion to Catholicism, and of the genesis of *Simplicissimus*) have been obliterated by time; and the authenticity of some texts (particularly the later editions of *Simplicissimus*) must still be questioned. Since it is quite possible that these matters will remain obscure forever, it is now the time simply to move forward as far as possible with what we have, and to seek ways of sum-totalling it all.

I have begun the book with a moderately detailed biography, partly because a thorough up-to-date account is lacking, and partly because I believe that the fragmentary documents make Grimmelshausen's extremely energetic and versatile personality shine through the surface and cast more light on his writings than is the case with most of his contemporaries. The analyses and interpretations of the works were conceived with the conviction of an all-pervading unity in the fictive world of the tales he unfolded ever anew in the brief span of eleven years. At the same time, an unbelievable variety and complexity was constantly manifested. Above all, I have striven to reveal and evaluate as fully as possible his incomparable and unique mastery of the art of storytelling.

KENNETH NEGUS

New Brunswick, N. J.

Acknowledgments

Acknowledgment is made here to the major Grimmelshausen scholars of this century, but particularly to Günther Weydt, author of the two most important recent books on Grimmelshausen, *Nachahmung and Schöpfung im Barock: Studien um Grimmelshausen* (1968) and *Hans Jacob Christoffel von Grimmelshausen* (1971); to the Research Council of Rutgers University for financial support in the initial stages of preparing this book; to Johannes Nabholz of Rutgers University for a helpful reading of the manuscript; to my graduate students (especially doctoral candidates) whose interest in Grimmelshausen and seventeenth-century German literature led to many valuable discussions in and outside of the classroom; to the editors of *The Astrological Review* for permission to incorporate portions of an article appearing in that journal into the section "The Children of the Planets" in Chapter Three; to Robert L. Hillyer and John C. Osborne, whose excellent translation of *Courasche* is quoted (all other translations are my own); and to Ulrich Weisstein, whose editorial counsel in the final stages of the book was invaluable. Finally to Joan Negus go my warm thanks for manifold assistance and patience during the writing of the book, and for typing the manuscript.

Contents

Chronology

1621 or 1622	Johann Jacob Christoph born in Gelnhausen. The best available evidence for his exact birthdate points to 1621 (March 17?).
ca. 1628– 1634	Attended school in Gelnhausen, under Lutheran supervision.
1634	The invasion and sacking of Gelnhausen by Imperial troops. The boy probably finds refuge in nearby Hanau, a well fortified Protestant stronghold.
1635	In the captivity of Croatians. Is subsequently recaptured by the Hessians and taken to Kassel.
1636	With Imperial troops at the siege and capture of Magdeburg. Participates in a campaign to the North (mainly in Westphalia) with a light cavalry regiment.
1638	With Imperial forces during the upper Rhine campaign.
1639– 1648	Musketeer, later clerk, in the regiment commanded by Reinhard von Schauenburg. Performs garrison duty in Offenburg (near Strasbourg). His conversion to Catholicism probably occurred during this period.
1648	Regimental Secretary under Freiherr von Elter. Takes part in Bavarian campaign.
1649	Married to Catharina Henninger.
1649– 1660	Stewardship under Schauenburg in Gaisbach. Acquisition of property. Various enterprises; innkeeper 1657–58.
1650– 1669	Births of his ten children.
1660– 1662	Has no official employment, but remains in Gaisbach.
1662– 1665	Steward and overseer of "Ullenburg," summer residence of the Strasbourg physician Johannes Küeffer.

1665–1667	Innkeeper of "The Silver Star" in Gaisbach.
1666	*Der satyrische Pilgram* I (*The Satirical Pilgrim* I) and *Der keusche Joseph* (*The Chaste Joseph*).
1667–1676	Mayor of the small town of Renchen.
1667	*The Satirical Pilgrim* II (along with I).
1668	*Simplicissimus* (first ed. in five books).
1669	Publication of *Die Continuatio* (*The Continuation* or Book VI of *Simplicissimus*, to which it is added in the second printing of the novel), and of *Der europäische Wundergeschichten-Calender* (*The European Calendar of Wondrous Tales*), an almanac.
1670	*Dietwald und Amelinde, Ratio Status, Lebensbeschreibung der Ertzbetrügerin und Landstörtzerin Courasche* (*Life History of the Archfraud and Runagate Courage*), *Der erste Beernhäauter* (*The First Sluggard*), *Die Wunderliche Gauckeltasche* (*The Strange Bag of Tricks*), *Musai* (appended to the second ed. of *The Chaste Joseph*), *Springinsfeld,* and the second *Calendar of Wondrous Tales.*
1671	*Der Ewig-während Calender* (*The Perpetual Calendar*), *Simplicissimus* (second and greatly altered edition; sometimes called the "Baroque" *Simplicissimus*), the third *Calendar of Wondrous Tales.*
1672	*Rathstübl Plutonis* (*Plutus' Council-Chamber*), *Die verkehrte Welt* (*The Topsy-Turvy World*), *Proximus und Lympida, Das wunderbarliche Vogelnest* I (*The Miraculous Bird's Nest* I), *Der stolze Melcher* (*Proud Melchior*), and the fourth *Calendar of Wondrous Tales.*
1673	*Der Bart-Krieg* (*The War of Beards*), *Der teutsche Michel* (*German Michael*), *Das Galgen-Männlin* (*The Mandrake*), and the fifth *Calendar of Wondrous Tales.*
1674	The sixth *Calendar of Wondrous Tales.*
1675	*The Miraculous Bird's Nest* II.
1676	Death on August 17.

CHAPTER 1

Grimmelshausen's Life

I The War and the Child

IN September, 1634, a horde of Croatian soldiers, serving the Catholic cause in the army of the Holy Roman Emperor, fell upon the small, predominantly Lutheran town of Gelnhausen in Hessia, east of Frankfurt am Main. With a savagery typical of the Thirty Years' War, they murdered most of the citizenry (numbering approximately fifteen hundred), tortured and drove off the rest, and plundered and burned until virtually a ghost-town was left behind. For decades to come, many of the houses in the town remained in ruins, including the one in which Hans Jacob Christoffel von Grimmelshausen had spent his childhood.

Gelnhausen, located in the fertile and prosperous valley called the "Wetterau," was only one of the many towns and villages upon which the Croatians (the Imperial soldiers most notorious for their brutality) and Spaniards had been unleashed after the Protestants' disastrous defeat at Nördlingen on September 6, 1634. A contemporary history describes this vast scene of madness in typical Baroque style:

Wherever they went, they filled heaven and earth with fire, smoke, fumes, blood, murder, shame and flame, suffering and outcry, so that it resounded unto the clouds and could not have been wrought or sounded worse; scarcely a town remained standing, no one dared to show himself, unless he wanted to die; or people stole into fortified places or into the thick underbrush, hills, forests, caves and clefts, among the dumb wild animals; but even then they were sometimes not safe, but were dragged out and—worse than if they were dumb animals—were beaten, shot, butchered, and torn to shreds, so that no tongue is so eloquent, no quill so sharp and pointed, that it could express and describe it fully. In sum, the land—before their arrival—was a joyful valley, a paradise and pleasure garden, and after their departure like a wild, deserted wasteland. . . .[1]

There followed the dreaded bubonic plague. Such was the world into which Grimmelshausen was suddenly plunged at about the age of thirteen. The Thirty Years' War had passed its midpoint the year before the attack and had long been moving along senselessly under its own power. The original issues of the conflict, both religious and political, were now hopelessly ensnarled and obscured. Huge armies lay sprawled across the German countryside, living off the land and propagating a brutal way of life that had become more and more accepted as inevitable. Among the civilian population of many towns, Armageddon seemed repeatedly to have descended, as it was so aptly rendered a few years later in Gryphius' most powerful poem about the war, the sonnet "Tears of the Fatherland: Anno 1636." With hyperbole piled on hyperbole, the poet describes how war, pestilence, conflagration, and death are visited upon the land, in seeming fulfillment of the prophecy of the Four Horsemen of the Apocalypse.

Precisely what happened to young Grimmelshausen and his family immediately after the sacking of Gelnhausen is unknown. They probably took refuge in Hanau, a well fortified town occupied by Protestant forces.[2] The commander of the fortress was Governor Ramsay, later presented as the main character's uncle in Books I and II of *Simplicissimus*. In any case, young Grimmelshausen was in all likelihood in Hanau by December, 1634. He undoubtedly suffered, too, from the extreme cold and hunger to which the many refugees in the town were subjected that winter.

Könnecke envisages what may well have happened in January, 1635. The bitter cold of this particular midwinter was such that the water in the moats surrounding the fortress was frozen solid, thus creating the ideal kind of place for thirteen-year-old boys to play, but at the same time eliminating a defense barrier. The enemy (again Croatians) took advantage of the ice, and, mounted on their swift horses, kidnapped young Grimmelshausen and some of his companions.

His captivity lasted only about a month, but must have left an indelible memory of misery, judging by the vividness and authenticity with which a similar episode in Simplicissimus' life is described (Book II, Ch. 13). The Croatians apparently used the boys for a variety of menial tasks in their crude encampments, and also made them assist in pillaging farms and villages. Even the regimental commander's, Colonel Corpus' (or Corpes'), manner of living was only slightly above that of an animal. The degradation suffered, and the atrocities witnessed, by the boys are reflected in the novel's poignant descriptions. Yet Grimmelshausen apparently could not conceal his admiration for a certain crude gallantry and military skill exhibited by this respected cavalry commander. Perhaps, the boy might have mused, the soldier's life was not so bad after all. The captivity soon ended, only to be replaced by another, around March 1, 1635, when he and at least some of his companions were captured by the Hessians, who held them for an unknown period in Kassel. (This episode is not reflected in *Simplicissimus*, but is mentioned later in *The Perpetual Calendar*.) The period of captivity, though possibly lasting for only a few months, may have severed his connections with home and family for years to come. The year following the spring of 1635 is a hiatus. Whether Grimmelshausen remained with the Hessians, whether he returned to Hanau and his grandfather (or uncle), escaped and hid in the woods, or was recaptured by Imperial forces is unknown to us. In any case, documentation is lacking up to the siege of Magdeburg in 1636. Then, at about the age of fifteen, he was in the field serving with the cavalry of the Imperial army.

II *Early Development*

Young Grimmelshausen had been torn from a home environment that was relatively secure and orderly, thought not without threats and actual attacks by military forces. In fact, in January, 1621 (possibly a few months before his birth) Spanish forces had caused severe damage to Gelnhausen. They then occupied it and the surrounding points for a full decade—until November, 1631, when the nearby fortress of Hanau was conquered and occupied by the Swedes. There followed three years of calm in the area, which remained under the control of friendly forces.

The child who grew up in these thirteen years of relative peace lived in a milieu that was unusual, but not without definite advantages. His father, Johannes, died when the boy was still a small child, and his mother, Gertraud, probably left young Hans behind in Gelnhausen when he was about six and remarried in nearby Frankfurt. It is assumed, then, that the boy spent his school years in the care of his paternal grandfather, who called himself Melchior Christoff (or Christoffel), and was a baker and innkeeper by trade. Melchior usually omitted the noble appendage, "von Grimmelshausen" from his name, although he was entitled to it.

Young Grimmelshausen must have attended his native town's only known school, whose curriculum and administration are described in detail in extant documents.[3] A child normally entered this elementary school at the of six or seven and attended it until about the age of twelve. Grimmelshausen was still a schoolboy at the time of the Croatian attack.[4] Beyond basic skills, there were three areas in which he had to be thoroughly trained. First, Lutheran religious indoctrination was heavily stressed, for the teaching and administration were handled mainly by the clergy. Thus the Luther Bible, catechism, and hymnal were basic texts of which one can find many verbal and other reminscences in Grimmelshausen's writings (in spite of his subsequent conversion to Catholicism). Secondly, musical education played an important role, primarily aimed at training choir boys and instrumentalists for religious observance. Both Simplicius' frequently mentioned musical ability and Grimmelshausen's musical sensibility in his verse suggest that the boy's musical talent had been developed to a high degree. Thirdly, Latin was taught from the first year on, and its use was increasingly encouraged. In the final years, the Latin classics were read in the original. Grimmelshausen may have missed the final stages of this level, for he seldom managed to avoid errors when using this language later in life.[5] It may have also become rusty through lack of use during the many years he spent in the war. Yet there is ample evidence at least of his having *read* a considerable amount of Latin.

A deep impression must have been made on him by the numerous trials and executions of witches in Gelnhausen which culminated in 1633 and 1634.[6] The jail where the witches were imprisoned almost bordered on the backyard of his grandfather's house. Persons accused of witchcraft must have been conducted by the authorities past the front of Melchior Christoff's house going to and from the jail. The trials, torturings, and beheadings of these unfortunates must have been a major topic of discussion for the townspeople, among whom must have circulated horrifying tales of witches' sabbats and esbats at the favorite haunt "under the pines" near the town; of "The Devil" who would have been the leader of a coven, and who enticed women into the forest, persuaded them to renounce God, and to participate in a travesty of the Baptism at a place called "The Sacred Well"; and of numerous acts of "black magic" committed by such persons. Grimmelshausen could well have been an eyewitness to witches' celebrations.[7] That such was his experience, leaving indelible impressions, is strongly supported by the major role played by witchcraft, black magic, and the Satanic in his writings. This realm of darkness is infernal evil distilled to its most fearsome extreme—the Cocytus of Grimmelshausen's inner world.

III   *The Aristocrat and the Burgher*

Grimmelshausen's upbringing was presumably the responsibility of his grandfather, Melchior Christoff. From the available documents there emerges a rather clear picture of a relationship, in which a fantastic vitality and versatility are passed on, skipping over the generation of the father, whom the boy could scarcely have remembered. Melchior Christoff exhibited a peculiar combination of character traits, probably stemming from his ambiguous social status as a man of noble lineage, having the prerogative of attaching "von Grimmelshausen" to his name, but choosing to omit it in most extant official documents. The name has been traced to a "Grimoldeshusen" line of landed nobles living in Thuringia during the Middle Ages. Könnecke's painstaking investigations reveal that some members of the family, though gradually becoming impoverished and déclassé, held positions of wealth in accordance with their heritage as late as the midsixteenth century. One of them was Georg Christoph von Grimmelshausen who had been the "Zentgraf," a kind of overseer, of a large area near Gelnhausen, and thus a man of considerable authority and apparently some property. That Georg von Grimmelshausen probably was Melchior Christoff's father.

Thus between the generation of our author's great-grandfather and that of his grandfather, the process of "Verbürgerlichung" or "burgherization" took place. Melchior von Grimmelshausen had cogent reasons to speed up the process by customarily dropping the "von Grimmelshausen" from his name, at the same time using "Christoff(el)" (apparently a middle name shared with his father) as a surname. He probably did this in order to win greater acceptability among his tradesmen peers.[8] Furthermore, he was, for his time at least, a kind of "radical," a leader of the minority faction of the city council, and evidently had hopes of breaking into the ruling circles. Hence he was willing to renounce what was otherwise a sign of distinction, for political advantage. He apparently induced his children to omit "von Grimmelshausen" from their names as well—to which they acquiesced, at least until after his death, at which time it was promptly tacked on again! Thus "What's in a name?"—along with seventeenth-century sociological implications—is a burning question in Grimmelshausen's background, and—as will be seen—in his later life and writings.

In all likelihood Melchior had inherited some property, but he was also, in part, a self-made man. He was by no means simply a baker. He probably was also the proprietor of an inn (as was occasionally the custom for bakers), and therefore needed a source of supply for wine, which was obtained in ever greater quantities from his own or rented vineyards, which he gradually acquired through his business acumen. He owned his own house and other extensive properties (such as farming plots and orchards). During the first two decades of the seventeenth century, he was a wealthy man reigning over a tiny economic dukedom of his own. Then there was a severe decline in his fortunes—doubtless caused mainly by the war—so that, at the time of his death (1640 or before), his debts exceeded the value of his estate. Melchior Christoff had run the full course of Fortuna's blessings and curses.

The personality of Melchior Christoff shines impressively through the fragmentary information on him that is available. He was obviously a talented and energetic man, often extremely aggressive and, in his zeal, capable of overstepping the boundaries of the ethical and social standards of his time. Yet otherwise he evidently practiced the principal virtues of his time, especially in the care of his family, and in his concern for public affairs. His rise and fall must have presented something reminiscent of a Baroque tragedy to the mind of his grandson, who may well have portrayed him in the hermit-father of his Simplicissimus, for the character and stature of this older man in the novel are more grandfatherly than fatherly.

IV "The Great God Mars"

In the dead center of Book I of *Simplicissimus*, the narrator, with grim picturesqueness, allegorically portrays the military machine, ruled by "the Great God Mars," as a rigidly structured society in itself. It is a hierarchy organized according to the various heights of the parts of a tree. He vividly depicts its extremes of tyranny, injustice, brutalization of its members, and arbitrary destructiveness. For well over a decade, following his captivity at about the age of thirteen, Grimmelshausen was to play several roles in this monstrous structure. Unlike the vast majority of those who started at the bottom, he managed eventually to scale the slippery trunk to a relatively secure and honorable height.

He could hardly have been an actual soldier when he appeared at Magdeburg, as from nowhere, in the late spring or summer of 1636, accompanying an army consisting of two encampments —a Saxon and an Imperial one—which were besieging the city.[9] He was, after all, no more than fifteen years old and, therefore, more likely to be one of the enormous body of noncombatants who accompanied armies in the seventeenth century. He was probably used as a forager in the surrounding area to alleviate the food shortage known to have existed in the camps. He may also have been a stableboy or orderly. Historically corroborated descriptions in Book II of *Simplicissimus* show Grimmelshausen's intimate knowledge of the soldier's life, as well as of the pitiful condition of the citizens and buildings of the city. Magdeburg suffered enormously in the war, its total destruction having been ordered by General Tilly in 1632, although it was not fully implemented. The remainder of the task was later all but completely carried out by others. It is symbolically significant that Grimmelshausen, author of the greatest novel about the war, should have been present in the city that probably suffered the worst of all those that were devastated in the three decades of the war.

In the fall, the Imperial and Saxon armies moved northward, eventually encountering the main force of the enemy, and were defeated at the bloody battle of Wittstock (October, 1636). Könnecke astutely compares the Wittstock episodes in *Simplicissimus* (Book II, Ch. 27) with historical documents and concludes that Grimmelshausen was *not* engaged in the battle itself, for there is a certain vagueness in the episode with respect to crucial factors in the strategy of the battle.[10] Futhermore, Grimmelshausen obviously refreshed his memory from a contemporary history book! Also a battle scene from Sidney's *Arcadia* appears to have been used as a source.[11] Yet he was definitely accompanying the army. It is, therefore, logical to assume that he was behind the battle lines with the noncombatants.

There is then a gap of at least a few months in the biographical documentation. At the end of 1636 or the beginning of 1637, the youth somehow became attached to a regiment of light cavalry assigned to the Imperial force commanded by the Bavarian Field Marshall, Baron Johann von Götz. The regiment arrived at its garrison in Soest (in Westphalia) in December, 1636. The unit was in the field for long periods during 1637, and young Grimmelshausen participated in at least some of the campaigns. Whether he fought as a soldier all or part of this time is unknown. It seems unlikely because of his youth; he was probably some kind of menial—very possibly a stableboy, since this was a cavalry unit. The area had suffered great damage from the war, so that even the armies were subject to food and fuel shortages in this formerly prosperous area. This was especially true of the fertile plain around Soest, which had been laid waste, much as had Grimmelshausen's homeland around Gelnhausen.

The light cavalry regiment was one of Götz's "Leibregimenter," i.e., it was under his personal command. Its members, therefore, enjoyed a prestige that they fully exploited. In fact, they were reported by Count von der Wahl, the Bavarian artillery commander, to be "the most insolent of soldiers," and were at times out of control, to the extent that extreme punishments, including torture and death, were inflicted on troublemakers (often to no avail). Wahl further reports that the officers were largely to blame for this lack of discipline.[12]

Here Grimmelshausen had ample opportunity to observe the living counterpart to the literary stock figure of the *miles gloriosus*, the vainglorious soldier resurrected from Roman times. The blending of life and literature takes place here in another way as well. For while the Hanau and Magdeburg episodes in *Simplicissimus* are, to a large extent, autobiographical, the Westphalian sections become more and more the novelist's inventions, even to the point of being fantastic. In fact, Simplicissimus' adventures in Books II and III (where he is the "Huntsman of Soest"), would seem to be the very opposite of the author's experiences there. The convent "Paradise" in Book II yields the best example. In the novel, Simplicissimus encounters there an improbable assemblage of "nuns"—charming young ladies of noble birth who are dazzled by his handsome appearance and musical talent. He further partakes of the famous Westphalian delicacies—ham, pumpernickel, and boiled beef. Beer and wine flow freely. He hunts on the convent grounds and learns how to fence. The whole episode is, then, designed to transform Simplicissimus into the dashing and "noble" figure that he is to cut for several chapters to come. Könnecke proves that nothing of the kind could have happened to Grimmelshausen at "Paradise," since the membership of its historical counterpart consisted of a few rather aged nuns. It was shielded from would-be intruders by strict rules and a severe prioress; and its general atmosphere would have been too austere to allow the goings-on depicted in the novel.[13]

In like manner, the other exaggerated pleasures enjoyed by the "Huntsman of Soest" are probably wish fulfillments of the author in retrospect. Grimmelshausen must have suffered hunger, cold, and many other discomforts. Although there had to be some opportunities for him to become such a connoisseur of Westphalian food (as Könnecke [14] so appetizingly proves), they must have been extremely rare. Furthermore, he may well not even have climbed onto the first rung of the military ladder as yet and, hence, probably felt himself to be in humiliating circumstances for the great-grandson of Georg Christoff von Grimmelshausen. In fact, once he became a full-fledged member of the military (perhaps in the following year) he remained a simple soldier (musketeer and cavalryman) for about five years. There is little evidence that he was the dashing leader of a military unit, mounted on horseback, living lavishly, and charming the ladies —all to the envy of soldiers and officers alike. It is improbable that he *ever* played such a role.

Yet in Westphalia he was at least a member of a more or less victorious army and could therefore have been in a somewhat more advantageous position than before. Soon, however, his fortunes took a turn for the worse. In the spring of 1638, Goetz moved most of his army to the Upper Rhine region, where

French and Protestant forces (having defeated Jan de Werth), were posing a threat, particularly to the key fortress of Breisach, which they were besieging. The Imperial attempt to relieve it and secure the area was a fiasco. Goetz, who turned out to be a mediocre strategist, engaged in long and complex maneuvers during the summer of 1638, but hesitated at critical points and failed to take advantage of positions of weakness on the part of his brilliant adversary, Count Bernhard of Saxe-Weimar. Goetz was decisively defeated at the battle of Wittenweier (August 8, 1638), and in November he was relieved of his command and replaced by Maximilian von der Goltz.

During that year, Grimmelshausen remained with the light cavalry, and perhaps actually became an active soldier in the winter or early spring. He served both as a "dragoon" ("Dragoner": a light cavalryman), and musketeer. He probably was constantly on the move with his regiment throughout the Upper Rhine area (Swabia, the Breisgau, Alsace, the Black Forest) and was present at Goetz's ignominious defeat at Wittenweier. He was also with the army in winter quarters (1938–39), after most of it had withdrawn eastward to the area of the Swabian-Bavarian border.

The events in *Simplicissimus* corresponding to those of the Upper Rhine campaign are distributed throughout Books IV and V, in a historically incorrect sequence, and they are interspersed with fictitious sections. Particularly noteworthy among the latter are: the whole Paris episode of Book IV; the long middle section of this book, dealing with Olivier; Simplicissmus' association with notorious "Marauder Brothers"; his service with the Protestant Neueneck Regiment; and the meetings and experiences with Hertzbruder. The corresponding period in Grimmelshausen's life was, in all probability, quite grim, and certainly dissimilar to the exciting and pleasant episodes depicted in the novel. One possible exception is constituted by a short stay in Switzerland in 1638.[15] He must have been frequently near this country's borders and may well have crossed it and observed conditions of peace just a few miles from war-torn Germany—a situation movingly described in Book V, Chapter 1 of the novel. Whether Grimmelshausen's conversion to Catholicism was associated with a similar visit to Switzerland in 1638, as reported in the novel, cannot be ascertained on the basis of extant evidence. Yet it is a possibility to be considered, since the episode is the most substantial source of information concerning this extremely important step in his life.[16]

The failures of Imperial and Bavarian forces in the Upper Rhine campaign left the area largely occupied by the Protestants and the French. Among the few regions retained in the midst of enemy-occupied territory was Offenburg, a town on the Rhine opposite, and to the south of, Strasbourg. After the fall of Breisach (December, 1638), the fortress of Offenburg soon became the strategic point of Imperial strength in the area. It retained this position for nine years, until the end of the war. This may have been due, in part, to a shift in the main action of the war to other theaters of operation, and partly to its able commander, Hans Reinhard von Schauenburg, a man held in high esteem by the Emperor, who was to remain Grimmelshausen's commander for most of the nine years to come, and subsequently his employer and benefactor.

We are relatively well informed about the conditions under which the inhabitants of Offenburg lived from 1639 to 1648. The town was almost constantly surrounded by the enemy, in varying degrees of besiegement and attack. Food and money were in short supply, as Schauenburg frequently mentioned in appeals for help to his superiors, even to the Emperor himself. The ensuing sufferings and discomforts caused significant numbers of soldiers to desert or behave rebelliously, thus undermining the effectiveness of the garrison, which was never large enough for its mission in the first place. Yet somehow it remained intact.

For young Grimmelshausen, however, this outwardly dismal garrison life proved to be a blessing in disguise, for here a turn of events occurred that had a direct bearing on his becoming a writer: he was appointed clerk in Schauenburg's headquarters, under the supervision of the Regimental Secretary, a well-educated man by the name of Johannes Witsch. It is not known exactly when this occurred, but it was not later than 1645, and probably around 1643.[17] In any case, Grimmelshausen remained in this post for three to five years.

These years probably provided an opportunity for continuing his education. His Gelnhausen schooling must have served him well as a preparation for the assignment. Johannes Witsch appears to have been instrumental in furthering the professional and mental growth of the young man who was now in his early twenties. Könnecke proves this with reference to the handwriting, in which Grimmelshausen closely followed his master.[18] The influence undoubtedly went further, for Witsch was a talented and respected man, on whom the signal honor of citizenship and high offices in Offenburg, which was not his native town, was later bestowed. The constant supervision, over several years, by such a man could scarcely have failed to accelerate the growth of this writer in the bud. Grimmelshausen was always fortunate in having support and patronage, earlier from his grandfather, and later from various members of the Schauenburg family.[19]

Unfortunately, the evidence for this formal education in Offenburg is largely circumstantial. We can assume that he had an opportunity to read a great deal; yet not a single author or title is mentioned in the sources in connection with this period. He may even have written some of the early parts of *Simplicissimus*.[20] He must also have developed his talent for drawing, shown by extant ink drawings, which are assumed to be his creations since the handwriting on them is his own.[21]

He must have found ever increasing favor among his superiors, for by the end of the war he had become the Regimental Secretary of a new commanding officer, Johann Burkhard Freiherr von Elter, who had previously been in Offenburg and was the brother-in-law of Hans Reinhard von Schauenburg. This assignment entailed a brief but definite change from garrison life to a fast-moving military campaign in Bavaria. This was the apex of his military career, and it was no slight responsibility. A regimental secretary at that time was the nerve center of the unit, with a special factor of responsibility: the commanding officer was generally far less adept with the pen than with the sword, hence his secretary often not only transcribed, but even composed official documents. Thus Grimmelshausen was a key member of the regimental staff, and as such received relatively high pay and allowances, including feed for two horses. He was, therefore, among the mounted personnel—a position of some prestige. Thus, for the first time, though not for long, he probably bore some resemblance to Simplicissimus in the role of the vainglorious Huntsman of Soest.

The part of the campaign in which he participated took place in the spring, summer, and autumn of 1648. Much of it consisted of withdrawing after initial defeats, maneuvering for position, and remaining in quarters awaiting battle. There was, however, ample opportunity to witness full-scale battle during a few engagements in the area of Munich, in May and June. Meanwhile, the Peace of Westphalia was being implemented, and the monstrous military machines of the Thirty Years' War slowly came to a halt, althought they were not yet disbanded. The Bavarian army retired to winter quarters (1648–49) with the prospect of soon being released. By the end of the winter, Grimmelshausen was no longer Regimental Secretary, for reasons unknown, but served with some unidentified unit of the Bavarian army.[22] He must have been discharged from military service in 1649. Thus he ended a period of fifteen years that he had spent in a predominantly military environment. He was about twenty-eight years old.

V   *Servant and Master*

After a war, young men marry and settle down. Grimmelshausen's wedding took place on August 30, 1649, and his duties as steward for the Schauenburg family began officially a week later, on September 7. His bride, Catharina Henninger, was the daughter of a lieutenant of the guard and sister of a musketeer, both serving in the Schauenburg regiment in Offenburg. It is reasonable to assume that the acquaintance with her and their courtship brightened Grimmelshausen's otherwise dreary garrison duty.

The Henninger family apparently enjoyed considerable prestige among the burghers of their native town, Zabern, where Catharina's father held important offices in the municipal government. A close relative, perhaps a brother of hers, was a Catholic clergyman. Aside from her religion, then, she was an appropriate wife for the grandson of Melchior Christoph. As for her personality, the same holds true: the energetic and versatile assistance she lent to her husband beyond the ordinary household duties is well-documented.[23] She bore him ten children during the first twenty years of their marriage; at least six of them lived to maturity.[24] She outlived her husband by seven years.

The transition from conditions of war to those of peacetime was relatively smooth for the young couple. Grimmelshausen's former commanding officer, Colonel Hans Reinhard von Schauenburg, became his principal employer. His new home was in the village of Gaisbach, near Oberkirch, which was not far from Offenburg, where he had spent nearly a decade as a soldier. His work as steward ("Schaffner") was mainly for Hans Reinhard, but he frequently performed various tasks for the latter's cousin, Carl, and other members of the family. He sometimes acted on behalf of individuals, at other times collectively for the whole Schauenburg family, with all its widespread branches and fiefs. (A similar position had been held by his great-grandfather, Georg Christoph von Grimmelshausen). The complexity of his responsibilities was increased by some additional factors: legal disputes between Hans Reinhard and Carl, poor economic conditions from the war, and the incredible variety of duties required of the steward. These years, at least up to 1665, must have been grimly demanding ones for the young husband and father, especially since he was not always duly rewarded for his services.

Yet Grimmelshausen's stewardship had its bright side, particularly as preparation for the future writer. His many talents were amply exercised and developed in this work, which also brought him into intimate contact with every conceivable activity in this microcosm of the Schauenburg estates. Much of his attention was focused on agricultural products such as wine, grain, poultry, cattle, and vegetables. Concern for the condition of the farmer in these difficult postwar year was added to his sympathy for their sufferings in the war.[25] He must have experienced mixed feelings when he, by no means rich himself, was required to collect rents in both money and goods, to supervise peasants in the rebuilding and replanting on farms devastated by the war, and to be, in general, the instrument of a stern law and authority that was sometimes wielded severely among these poor folk whose sad plight had not ended with the war.

Grimmelshausen's practical talents further served him in the construction of many buildings, and in interior decoration. He apparently had a highly developed visual sense, especially for spatial relationships, which had already manifested itself in his drawings of the fortifications at Offenburg, and his ink reproduction of the castle of Geroldseck. Now he helped design buildings and supervised their construction.[26] He also painted the interior of a summer house (ornamentally) for Anna Walpurga von Schauenburg and received the handsome sum of fifteen florins for his service. Related to such work would also be his position as verger of the Schauenburgs' private chapel in Gaisbach. He had, then, a modest claim to some ability in the visual arts and crafts—a talent later employed for his own significant illustrations to his writings.[27]

Accompanying such relatively colorful activities was the dreary and exacting task of keeping accounts, some of which have been preserved. These documents make up a large part of the biographical sources for this period. The reckoning was mainly in amounts of goods, but some money was also involved. Grimmelshausen seems to have performed this function well, at least in a technical sense. He revised the system of his predecessor for greater clarity; and extreme precision is everywhere apparent. Perhaps these characteristics were fostered by at least one of his employers, Hans Reinhard, who was an exacting auditor at the end of each fiscal year (Sept. 7). The accounting system reveals certain peculiarities that are puzzling, particularly for assessing Grimmelshausen's honesty. He seems to have had unspecified privileges in using the capital of money and goods which were entrusted to him. Thus he frequently borrowed from them for his own personal use, or for investment in his own private business dealings, such as real estate (especially mortgages), wine, and horses.[28] Some of the amounts involved were not repaid— at least not by the annual day of reckoning. Instead, they were simply carried over as "outstanding," vaguely accountable to a future date, since there were apparently no clear rules governing such (mis-?) appropriations. The result was that, in the first five years, there was a dramatic increase of his debt to his employer's capital. In 1655 a crisis seems to have arisen. The details are unknown, but it seems probable that Grimmelshausen's employment was in jeopardy. He continued to act as overseer, however. There was an agreement that he repay the amounts in arrears. At about the same time he took on the additional tasks of tavern keeper. It is reasonable to assume that he desperately needed additional income for his rapidly growing family, now including as many as five children. A probable long-range result of this episode is his near-obsession with money, which emerges at important points in his writings (*Simplicissimus*, Book III, and *Ratstübl Plutonis*).

During the Gaisbach period, Grimmelshausen wrote a considerable number of official letters, legal documents, and the like in connection with his duties. His high degree of literacy must have been a major asset, especially since Hans Reinhard was no exception among his peers, who were relatively illiterate. Undoubtedly the same applies to Karl Reinhard's cousin Carl, who, in addition, was so "frenchified" that his written German would have been even worse than Hans Reinhard's.[29] Thus Grimmelshausen's secretarial duties went far beyond the taking of dictation; they even included the drafting of important legal documents, letters, and the like.[30] Such writings were properly composed in the florid, elevated style of the time.[31] Equally, if not more, important are the less sophisticated records and notes dealing with the details of everyday life and thus lending a certain realistic capability to his power as a writer. Thus Grimmelshausen's practical, like his social background, encompassed matters ranging from the patrician to the plebeian level. In a strange way, his position as innkeeper (1656–58) combined similar antitheses. The serving of food and beverages to the people of Gaisbach can hardly be characterized as patrician. Yet it was made possible by the bestowal of a kind of fief on him by Philipp Hannibal von Schauenburg, a man of about Grimmelshausen's age, who shared the innkeeper's sense of humor and his interest in literature. Philipp Hannibal was later to become Grimmelshausen's literary patron and the member of the Schauenburg family with whom relations were most cordial. There was even some literary collaboration between them.[32]

The property consisted of a house, farm buildings, and arable land. The house, however, had lain in ruins since the war and had to be rebuilt under the new occupant's supervision, who wished, at the same time, to make it suitable as a tavern. Thus again Melchior Christoff, who had probably been an innkeeper, was reincarnated in his grandson. Grimmelshausen's close familiarity with inns resulted, later on, in some of his most impressive folk scenes, such as the inn episode at the beginning of *Springinsfeld.*

Unfortunately, this added source of income failed to extricate Grimmelshausen from his ever worsening financial predicament. The inn could hardly have been a goldmine, since it was one of two serving the tiny village of Gaisbach. He gave it up in 1658, without having repaid the aforementioned arrears. In fact, toward the end of the decade, the Schauenburgs' expenditures in money and goods exceeded their income. It is impossible to determine whether this was caused in part by Grimmelshausen's mismanagement (if there was any). In any case, his employment was terminated, and he was officially succeeded by a new overseer on September 7, 1660.[33] He did not leave Gaisbach immediately, however, but continued to carry out occasional tasks for the Schauenburgs, with whom he remained on sufficiently cordial terms to invite Reinhard's wife, Johanna Walpurga, to be godmother to one of his children (1663) and namesake (perhaps also godmother) of another around 1664 or 1665. He was obliged, nonetheless, to seek new employment in 1660. He did not succeed in finding it until 1662.

His new employer was a wealthy physician, Dr. Johannes Küeffer, son of a Strasbourg physician by the same name, who had begun the family's ascent toward aristocracy. Johannes the younger continued on this path, as is indicated by his acquisition of the "Ullenburg," a castle on a hilltop north of Gaisbach. Grimmelshausen's duties here were much the same as those performed as steward for the Schauenburgs, but with the additional ones of "Burgvogt" (castle caretaker). Probably his work was less complicated and time-consuming, especially since the Ullenburg was primarily Küeffer's summer residence.

There is evidence of much dissatisfaction with the new employer on Grimmelshausen's part. In *Simplicissimus* (Book IV, Ch. 1–6), the author portrays a physician in a social position so similar to that of Küeffer's that there can be little doubt that he was the model. (There are no other physicians known to have played such an important role in Grimmelshausen's life.) Not only does Grimmelshausen bestow the uncomplimentary name of "Dr. Canard" on him, but he also portrays him as unscrupulous, cruel, conceited, and sometimes downright silly in his concern for outward appearances. He is, in other words, the caricature of a social climber.

There is, however, another aspect of this three-year period with Küeffer (1662–1665) that contributed much toward Grimmelshausen's first major phase of literary production. Parts of his first two published books, *The Satirical Pilgrim* and *The Chaste Joseph* could have been written at that time. Indeed, it appears that the Ullenburg years provided a major impetus toward his becoming a full-fledged writer (about 1665). Dr. Küeffer was keenly interested in all the arts, especially literature. He even wrote some verse himself. Probably the most important factor, however, was Küeffer's acquaintance with literary figures in and around Strasbourg—including Jesaias Rompler von Löwenhalt, Johann Matthias Schneuber, and (most significant for Grimmelshausen) the Alsatian satirist Johann Michael Moscherosch.[34] Grimmelshausen's feelings toward this part of the contemporary literary world—the only part with which he is known to have had close contact—were mixed. Most negative were his views concerning the Strasbourg "Upright Fir-Tree Society" ("Aufrichtige Tannengesellschaft") as well as toward other similar literary-linguistic societies. His scorn was aroused particularly by the excesses in the linguistic reforms proposed by these groups. Their puristic, over-sophisticated, and often bloodless, products and projects were foreign to his nature. Only Moscherosch, author of the satirical *Visions of Philander von Sittewald* (*Gesichte des Philanders von Sittewald*) could provide the major precedent and some of the impetus for his own satire.

Grimmelshausen apparently carried out his duties conscientiously at the Ullenburg; at least the few pertinent documents available indicate this.[35] Yet, again, he chose, or was forced to, give up his employment there, after about three years of service. The reasons are unknown. Whatever their nature, a considerable store of bitterness, often voiced, toward all that Küeffer represented was evident in Grimmelshausen's writings for the remaining eleven years of his life. To a degree, this constituted a rebellion against the whole literary establishment of the German Baroque.[36]

Between 1665 and 1667 Grimmelshausen was again without official employment, and again he took recourse to earning a living as innkeeper. This time, his tavern was located on the so-called "Spithalbühne," a piece of property in Gaisbach he had acquired in 1653, and on which he had built two houses. He named his inn "The Silver Star"—possibly in reminiscence of "The Golden Star," the probable name of Melchior Christoph's inn in Gelnhausen.[37] There is no reason to regard this second period of innkeeping as more successful than the first. There is, however, a major difference: Grimmelshausen made his name as a writer while in this humble occupation. For during these two years he completed *The Satirical Pilgrim* and *The Chaste Joseph*,[38] and wrote a large part, perhaps over half, of *Simplicissimus*.[39]

In 1667, Grimmelshausen, now in his midforties, was appointed to an office that was eminently suited to his abilities and experiences. He was appointed mayor of the small town of Renchen (in the bishopric of Strasbourg), located downstream on the Rench River from the Gaisbach and Ullenburg area. At first he was unable to post the required bond. Then an alternate arrangement was made: his property in Gaisbach was accepted as partial security (valued at 400 to 500 florins), and his father-in-law posted the remainder.

His duties as mayor were many and various. Now, however, he seems to have enjoyed more prestige than when his versatility was exploited in his stewardships. There is weighty evidence that in Renchen he was treated with respect and admiration by the townspeople and had to endure little or none of the humiliation that he must have suffered in Gaisbach and at Ullenburg. Simplicissimus, often a self-portrait, undergoes a radical character change in the sequels to *Simplicissimus* that were written in Renchen. The chameleonlike, easily corruptible picaresque hero of before (especially in *Springinsfeld*) becomes a morally impeccable, solemn, and impressive middle-aged man, playing a consistently commanding role in all situations, often as a kind of seer and and sage, and treated with deference by all. In Renchen, in other words, Grimmelshausen became the person described by the priest who wrote his death certification: "an honorable man and possessing great talent and erudition."

His responsibilities included such things as tax-collecting; the preparation of contracts and other legal documents relating to every phase of life in the community (marriage, inheritance, property, etc.); the inspection and maintenance of standards in agricultural and other goods and services; law enforcement (including arrests, and the exclusion of thieves and beggars from the town); and some dispensation of justice (such as levying fines for minor offenses). Limited as this small-town environment must have been, he was still in a position to observe its citizens intimately and deeply. He could well have envisioned himself as resembling the invisible bearers of the miraculous bird's nest (the invention of his final work), who were often secret witnesses to the evil and folly of persons falsely believing that they were committing their wrongs undetected.

The brief nine years as mayor were also Grimmelshausen's most productive period as writer. The enormous volume of his writings at this time is all the more impressive when one considers the adverse conditions under which he lived during the war that raged through the Renchen area during the last three years of his life. After completing *The Satirical Pilgrim, The Chaste Joseph,* and *Simplicissimus* (Books I through V) by 1667, he immediately went on to the Simplician sequel (Book VI), entitled simply *Continuation* (1669). Then, in his remaining years, appeared Books VII through X, comprising the last four sequels, entitled *The Runagate Courage* (1670), *Springinsfeld* (1670), and Parts I and II of *The Miraculous Bird's Nest* (1672 and 1675, resp.). Interspersed were the two idealistic "heroic-gallant" novels, *Dietwalt and Amelinde* (1670) and *Proximus and Lympida* (1672); *The Perpetual Calendar* (1671); other calendars; and a variety of shorter pieces. The peak of creativity was reached at the end of the 1660's, for in 1670 no fewer than *six* (perhaps seven) books by him were published.[40] *Simplicissimus,* by far the most popular, went through five subsequent editions, as did a few others, within their author's lifetime. The great volume of writing may have been due in part to pressure from his publisher, Felssecker, who could well have been exploiting the popularity of *Simplicissimus* to the point of great strain—or even a break—between the two men.[41] The quality of the writing remained, nonetheless, remarkably high.

A tragic irony underlies this period of artistic fruition. The bitter pills that may have been meted out to him by Grimmelshausen's publisher were a trifle by comparison with what the course of history had in store for him. For this man, who had suffered so intensely from war in his youth, was not to enjoy peace in his final years—a peace that had just begun to promise him and his countrymen a life that was free from the extreme privations of the Thirty Years' War and its aftermath. From 1673 on, Renchen and vicinity were the scene of the same kind of devastation and misery that he knew only too well. Again troops (French and Imperial) were quartered in the towns, again they destroyed and plundered, foraged and exacted tributes, and brought with them the usual starvation and pestilence. As

mayor, Grimmelshausen was in the difficult position of representing his townspeople in negotiations with his superiors in
Strasbourg, both in damage claims and in connection with
tributes exacted for the Imperial "allies" occupying Renchen. In
the course of the next three and a half years, the state of affairs
sank to an abysmal low, particularly when demands were made
by the military for supplies that were either nonexistent or pitifully depleted. Such conditions prevailed to the very day of
Grimmelshausen's death, on August 17, 1676.

His death certificate in the Renchen church records is one of
the most valuable extant documents for Grimmelshausen, and is
therefore translated here in full from the original Latin:

Deceased: an honorable man and one of great talent and erudition,
Johannes Christoph von Grimmelshausen, mayor of this town; and although—because of the disturbances of the war—he had enlisted in the
military [militia?], and his sons [children?] had thereafter been scat-
tered all about, nonetheless all by chance came together here; and the
parent, strengthened by the holy sacrament of the Eucharist, expired
and was interred. May his soul rest in sacred peace.[42]

The high esteem in which Grimmelshausen was held (for his
"honorableness," talent and erudition) is obvious at the beginning. In addition to this, there is a definite touch of warmth
conveyed in the official Latin of the clergyman writing the
entry. Secondly, a totally new fact emerges here: military service had *not* ended for Grimmelshausen in Offenburg in 1649,
but now in his midfifties he again was obliged to take up arms.
The exact nature of this service is unknown. It may have been
with the Imperial regiment of Max von Fürstenberg, which was
in the vicinity at the time, and in which Grimmelshausen's son,
Franz Joseph Ferdinand is known to have later served. The unit
may also have been a citizens' militia, organized to protect the
citizenry from both hostile and "friendly" forces. In any case,
here emerges another dreary and horrible episode in the history
of seventeenth-century warfare. Thirdly, the Grimmelshausens'
family life must have been severely disrupted, to the extent that
the various members members were separated from each other
—possibly in order to bring the young ones to safety, while the
older sons served in the military.[43] It was only by accident
("casu") that the sons (or all the children) were able to be

with their father in his final hours. Finally, the document reveals the fact that Grimmelshausen died in the Catholic faith, into which the fortunes of war had brought him and which now, again in war, offered him his last solace.

CHAPTER 2

Sources and Beginnings

I *Literary Convention and the Lonely Outsider*

GRIMMELSHAUSEN portrayed his times with the aura and
and detail of a realism in which he surpassed all his contemporaries. Upon surveying his life it is apparent that this was
an outgrowth of his intense and varied experience. Yet it is also
known (and obvious) that his memory stored a vast amount of
material derived from reading, and that extensive literary borrowings were blended with the autobiographical elements to form
organic wholes that often defy attempts to distinguish between
life and art. Some of the most "lifelike" scenes were derived
from books, while others showing less verisimilitude are demonstrably biographical![1] Thus certain materials derived from tradition, though disguised as contemporary life, can be traced through
his works. In varying degrees this is true of all writers: but it
should be stressed in the case of Grimmelshausen, who for decades was thought (erroneously) to have simply retold in *Simplicissimus* a slightly altered version of his early life.[2]

A complicating factor in placing Grimmelshausen into the
literary history of his time is his relative independence from
the other principal figures. The ruling literary potentates and
circles owed their place largely to Martin Opitz (1597–1639),
who, near the time of Grimmelshausen's infancy, single-handedly
determined much of the course of German literature—especially
in theory—for decades to come with his *Book on German Poesie*
(*Buch von der deutschen Poeterey*) of 1624. Opitz's aim was
nothing less than a total reform of his nation's literature and
literary language on the basis of classical and certain contemporary foreign models. He proposed strict rules of prosody, genre,
and moral didacticism. The poet as aristocrat is implied throughout. This latter idea was supported by the *Sprachgesellschaften*
—literally "linguistic societies"—which, however, concerned them-

selves with literary and general cultural matters as much as with language reform. Both Opitz and the *Sprachgesellschaften* received considerable support from the courts, and therefore tended to regard German folk culture and its literature as vulgar and irrelevant to their programs.

Grimmelshausen's only known close contact with a member of a *Sprachgesellschaft* was with Dr. Küeffer of the "Upright Fir-Tree Society" of Strasbourg.[3] As was pointed out, this relationship probably left much antipathy in Grimmelshausen's mind toward all things associated with Küeffer. Further opposition to this society and similar ones emerged later in full force in *The German Michael* (1673), in which he attacks both the excessive purism and the unnecessary use of foreign words. His most impressive statement on the subject is that concerning the very prototype of the German *Sprachgesellschaften*, the "Fruit-Bearing Society" ("Fruchtbringende Gesellschaft"). With a brilliant metaphorical conceit, Grimmelshausen compares this illustrious company to a caravan of jackasses and mules, transporting oranges, lemons, and pomegranates northward over the Alps.[4] This "Fruit-Bearing Society" included the most famous German authors of the time: Martin Opitz, Andreas Gryphius, Philipp von Zesen, Georg Philipp von Harsdörffer, Hans Michel Moscherosch, Adam Olearius, Johann Rist, and many others.

Grimmelshausen's criticisms were, however, directed primarily at those *linguistic* reforms that he considered excessive, unnatural, and senseless. As far as literature is concerned, there were a few points at which he and at least some of the above authors agreed. His debt to Moscherosch was very great indeed, as will be shown. Olearius' *Travels to the Orient* was used extensively as a source for Simplicissimus' journeys. There is evidence that Harsdörffer—unmatched in refined superficiality—contributed substantially to *Simplicissimus*.[5] And Grimmelshausen at least attempted in some of his minor works to cultivate one genre of the Opitzian tradition—the aristocratic novel. As in life, Grimmelshausen was, at times, an aristocrat in literature, but he usually managed to avoid the attendant dangers of the contemporary "baroque" style—vacuousness, bombast, and preciosity.

It is a curious fact of literary history that during the very time of the writing of Grimmelshausen's works—the 1660's and the 1670's—these extremes of the baroque style were in full bloom among Opitz's literary progeny. These decades were dominated by the Silesians, Christian Hofmann von Hofmannswaldau (1617–1679), Daniel Casper von Lohenstein (1635–1683), and minor figures under their aegis. For over two centuries to follow, these were the authors who, in the minds of the German reading public, represented all that was most characteristic for this century. Theirs was an art depicting extreme tensions between antithetical themes (such devices as the oxymoron being favored), incredible self-indulgence in exaggeration and bombast, and toying with empty word games and conceits. Whether such a characterization is just or unjust, cannot be argued in this context.[6] It must suffice here to assert at least that this late Silesian school, prime representatives of "High Baroque," was even further removed spiritually from Grimmelshausen than it was geographically. Thus Koschlig writes:

We know that Grimmelshausen was completely self-taught, having no personal contact with the predominant minds of his time. Literarily he was a lonely outsider, receiving no assistance whatsoever from the *Sprachgesellschaften*.[7]

II *Satire*

Continuing from the above, Koschlig states:

From Scholte's source studies, however, we also know the extent to which Grimmelshausen knew how to enrich his autobiographical storehouse with fruits of reading in quantities . . . that are unimaginable by today's standards.

That he did not write primarily in the tradition of Opitz certainly does not mean that he was without literary precursors and contemporaries who influenced him. Grimmelshausen clearly followed in the footsteps of a series of authors reaching as far back as the fifteenth century. These were representatives of the still-emerging middle class who cultivated an unsophisticated body of literature, always didactic (at least professedly so), but also rough-hewn and bawdy, with a large dosage of humor and satire. The main figures of this tradition who prefigure Grimmelshausen are Sebastian Brant (1458–1521), Hans Sachs (1494–1576), Johann Fischart (1546–1590) and Hans Michel Moscherosch (1601–1669). In the seventeenth century, this tradition, whose satirical element is of particular concern here,[8] survived largely outside Opitzian circles, in spite of Moscherosch's membership in the Fruit-Bearing Society.[9]

The major German satire immediately preceding *Simplicissimus* is unquestionably Moscherosch's *Strange and True Visions of Philander von Sittewald* (Part I: 1640; Part II: 1643). Strongly derivative in its first several "visions" from Quevedo, Moscherosch, while writing the book, gradually departed from his Spanish model, so that Part II is wholly his own creation. There is also a progression from a universal kind of satire in the beginning, to attacks on peculiarly German problems in Part II. The dream visions of human folly and vanity (at first all mankind's, then Germany's) are presented in more or less arbitrary sequence, the main unifying factor being Philander, first as an observer, then as a participant in the action. Part II is of special interest here, for two major elements of it had a perceptible impact on *Simplicissimus*. The first vision of this part satirizes the so-called "Alamode" culture of seventeenth-century Germany. This was a culture imported mainly from France and manifesting itself largely in flamboyant styles of clothing and hairdress (the men wore their hair long and curled), and in the excessive use of foreign words (especially French). In opposing such things, Moscherosch embraces the viewpoint of the German burgher, whose simple and conservative tastes were in sharp contrast to these customs superimposed upon German life, partly through the gallicized courts (with some Italian influence as well), and partly due to the presence of foreign armies during the war. Grimmelshausen's ridicule of these things reaches a climax where Simplicius plays the socially critical "fool" in Book II of *Simplicissimus*.

The second major satirical element adapted from *Philander von Sittewald* concerns the portrayal of the soldier in the Thirty Years' War. The *miles christianus* is shown here to have deteriorated into the swashbuckling, blustering *miles gloriosus*—the type whose most famous comical portrayal of the century is found in Gryphius' *Horribilicribrifax*. Simplicius exemplifies this type when he becomes the swaggering Huntsman of Soest. In *Philander von Sittewald,* as well as in other passages of *Simplicissimus,* this figure is also presented as a sadist in the treatment of captives. The impact of Moscherosch is also observable in the important dream and visionary episodes employed for purposes of satire and criticism in *Simplicissimus, The Topsy-Turvy World,* and Book VI (the *"Continuation"*); in the use of dialect and colloquialisms; and in countless details.[10] This literary relationship may well have been only part of their association: there were a number of occasions on which the two writers could have had personal contact, and it is certain that they had at least one mutual acquaintance: Dr. Küeffer,[11] and probably another by the name of Antoni Freiherr von Lützelburg.[12]

In any case, Moscherosch—significantly the most important German satirist immediately preceding Grimmelshausen—had the most perceptible and extensive impact on him of any single writer of his generation. And it is as a *satirist* that Grimmelshausen plays the most clear-cut role in the literary history of his century. No more appropriate motto could be used to convey this fact than the little verse on the title page of the later editions of *Simplicissimus*:

> Es hat mir so wollen behagen
> Mit Lachen die Wahrheit zu sagen.
> (I simply felt disposed
> To tell the truth with a laugh.)

III   *The Developmental, Picaresque, and Aristocratic Novel*

Simplicissimus is often considered to be in the tradition of the "developmental novel" (*Entwicklungsroman*) and its related forms.[13] This typically German genre extends from the medieval epic *Parzival* of Wolfram von Eschenbach through Wieland's *Agathon,* Goethe's *Wilhelm Meister,* several novels of the Romantic period, Keller's *Green Henry,* and into our century (Hermann Hesse's *Glass-Bead Game* and Thomas Mann's *Doctor Faustus*). The complexity and controversial nature of this form, and its bearing on *Simplicissimus,* preclude a complete discussion here. Much is a matter of definition. It must suffice to point out that *Simplicissimus* has one simple feature in common with the works of this German novel tradition: it tells a lifestory from childhood to maturity. Furthermore, it bears a definite resemblance in many details to its great predecessor, *Parzival.* (A fifteenth-century edition of this courtly epic is known to have been available in a library to which Grimmelshausen had access.[14])

Certain elements of *Simplicissimus*, especially in the opening episodes, reveal a similarity to this epic that is clearly more than coincidental. These include: the hero's early upbringing in isolation from society; his naiveté as a child; the initial inadequacy of his early religious training; his fright upon first viewing horses at a relatively late stage of childhood; and certain common features of the hermit figures.[15] If, however, Grimmelshausen was influenced by a reading of Wolfram's epic, he considerably modified much of the material. This suggests that the adaptations are partly or wholly subconscious reminiscences.

Much closer to Grimmelshausen chronologically is the rogue's, or picaresque, novel that was at a peak of popularity in Germany during the author's lifetime.[16] Spanish in origin, the most significant specimens of this genre are the anonymous *Lazarillo de Tormes* (1553); Alemán's *Guzmán de Alfarache* (1599); Ubedá's *La pícara Justina* (1605); Cervantes' *Rinconete y Cortadilla* (1613); and Charles Sorel's *Histoire comique de Francion*. Grimmelshausen could have read all of these works in German versions, some of which had been greatly altered by the translators. The details and the extent of their influence are matters of considerable speculation, much of which has yielded mainly negative or vague results.[17] It is apparent enough on the surface that Simplicissimus, to a degree, is a "roguish" hero, and thus related to those of the above-mentioned works. Such features as his lower-class origins, swift-moving adventures, clever pranks, the sequence of relationships with various character types (especially his "masters"), the vacillations of his fortunes, the conclusion of his wanderings and his settling down at the end— these all combine to place *Simplicissimus* at least partially within the history of this subgenre of the European novel. Furthermore, Grimmelshausen also created a *feminine* "rogue" figure in *Courasche,* as did Ubedá in the above-mentioned *Justina.* As with Simplicius, however, Courasche's literary genealogy remains uncertain.

Formerly it seemed unquestionable that Grimmelshausen borrowed whole passages almost verbatim from the translation and revision of Alemán's *Guzmán de Alfarache* by Aegidius Albertinus, "the father of the German picaresque novel."[18] Scholte then proved that the verbal correspondences were the result of a complex process involving sources used by both Albertinus and

Grimmelshausen, and that Grimmelshausen's immediate source was actually a nonliterary one (Garzoni, to be discussed later). This left unanswered the question of Grimmelshausen's debt to the most likely literary predecessor of Simplicissimus as *pícaro*. A few borrowings from Albertinus' *Guzman* are still within the realm of possibility.[19] It is unlikely that Grimmelshausen would not have read any Spanish picaresque novels, popular and accessible as they were.[20] Furthermore, publications by Albertinus (other than *Guzman*) were among his favorite source works.[21] Yet, one must admit, no extensive and completely convincing evidence for a more or less direct influence of the Spanish *novela picaresca* has so far been uncovered.

There is at least one piece of solid evidence in this gray zone of uncertainty. This is the definite influence of Charles Sorel's *Comical History of Francion* on Grimmelshausen.[22] As Koschlig has shown, Grimmelshausen derived a variety of important features from this French novel, through which at least an *indirect* influence of *Lazarillo de Tormes* and *Guzmán de Alfarache* was channeled to Grimmelshausen. It is probable that *Francion* is the main source of the character Jupiter in Book III of *Simplicissimus*,[23] and of the Hertzbruders. Indeed, the reading of this book around 1665 or 1666 could well have acted as a catalyst that set off the creation of *Simplicissimus*, after Grimmelshausen's first, and relatively unsuccessful attempts at writing immediately preceding that time. The main elements of the satirical *style*—of "telling the truth with a laugh"—may, indeed, have been learned more from Sorel than from Moscherosch. Furthermore, a special concept of "wholeness" ("Vollkommenheit") as a goal of the novelist was demonstrably adapted by Grimmelshausen to form an even greater and more coherent work of literary architecture than *Francion*. Thus the problem of Grimmelshausen's sources of the "picaresque" is complicated by the modifications of a French author, and by the largely indirect path by which the Spanish *pícaro* probably reached the Gaisbach innkeeper.

A third literary tradition—that of the "heroic-gallant" novel— is less extensive in Grimmelshausen's better-known works than is that of the satirical and picaresque. Yet it is represented in his career as writer, especially toward the beginning. Most important, it plays a clearly major role in *Simplicissimus*. This tradition, introduced to Germany by Opitz's translation (1626) of

John Barclay's *Argenis*, dominated the conventional German Baroque novel, reaching a stage of incredible excesses in length and complexity during the end of that period.[24] The main characters were typically young lovers of noble birth, whose story consists of a series of episodes in which all manner of barriers to their union are created up to their final joyful reunion. Idealization of the virtues of such persons, in their aristocratic roles, was the rule. Some veiled commentary on contemporary politics, however, was frequently included. Suspense was created by the withholding of important information from the reader, or by the creation of false impressions; but these were removed toward the end with various forms of revelations and recognitions, leading to the lovers' permanent bliss. Grimmelshausen wrote two such "heroic-gallant" novels: *Dietwald and Amelinde* (1670) and *Proximus and Lympida* (1672). Definite features of the genre are also present in *Joseph the Chaste* (1666) and *Ratio Status* (1670). Finally, as will be seen, both the theme and the structure of *Simplicissimus* are affected in an important way as a result of the hero's noble birth, carrying with it the elements of this aristocratic form of the novel—as foreign as it may seem both to Grimmelshausen's character and *Simplicissimus*.

It is apparent that several different currents of literary influences converged on Grimmelshausen. As will be seen, none of these provides an adequate category for describing his literary production as a whole, nor any single work, even the most conventional. It was Grimmelshausen's role as a writer to synthesize and transcend the past and the present.

IV *Nonliterary sources*

The book that provided Grimmelshausen with the greatest number of authoritative quotations and allusions was a German translation of Thomas Garzoni's *Piazza Universale* (Frankfurt a/M, 1619), a book describing all known "professions, arts, businesses, trades, and crafts." This German edition was provided with robustly realistic illustrations derived from the sixteenth-century woodcuts of Jost Ammann.[25] Scholte more than adequately proves the ubiquitous presence of this book in Grimmelshausen's writings.[26] Most derivations involve factual material, but it is important to note that this is a considerable part of the realistic texture of his works, since it concerns mainly the tangibles of everyday life. Furthermore, the Ammann illustrations are remarkably similar in style to those made by Grimmelshausen for *Simplicissimus*.[27]

A second source in a related category is Johannes Colerus' basic reference work on agriculture, entitled *Oeconomia ruralis et domestica,* the most popular book of its kind in the seventeenth and eighteenth centuries.[28] Mainly of interest as a source for *The Perpetual Calendar* of 1670, the derivations from Colerus serve Koschlig to explode the myth that Grimmelshausen was a "farmer's writer." For, as he demonstrates, much of the agricultural lore in Grimmelshausen's writings that has the flavor of personal experience is, in fact, taken bodily from Colerus! Also Grimmelshausen's editorial emendations of Claus von Schauenburg's *Der Teutsche Friedens-Raht* (1670), a book dedicated to the administration of landed estates, show that Grimmelshausen carried out the task with Colerus as his guide. Grimmelshausen, then, regarded farming and the peasantry from the aloof point of view of a nobleman, informing himself about them largely from books.

There are many more nonliterary sources, Grimmelshausen's reading being unbelievably extensive. Kissel attempts to list them all, but without indicating their relative importance.[29] Other attempts have been made to exhaust materials of lesser importance, such as saints' tales.[30] It is altogether conceivable that still more important findings will be made in this area of source-studies.

It should be noted that in the enormous amount of "borrowings" from the writings of others (a more acceptable custom then than now), Grimmelshausen seldom copied entire passages verbatim. Both Scholte and Koschlig[31] have analyzed his revisions of these texts—ranging from small and subtle stylistic emendations to total recastings of entire sentences and paragraphs. Thus we are given insights of an intimate nature into Grimmelshausen's manipulation of language. One of his most common alterations was to provide a borrowed passage with a livelier context than it had originally had. The best example is the lengthy passage from Garzoni included in *The Perpetual Calendar* where Garzoni's rather wooden discussion concerning prophecy is imbued with considerable vitality by converting it into a dialogue between Simplicissimus and Garzoni. Another method is to establish an I-Thou relationship between the author and the reader. Sometimes details from Grimmelshausen's own experience are injected. In matters of grammar and syntax we encounter such changes as deletion of infelicitous repetitions; more euphonius wordings; clarifications; omissions of unnecessary words; improvements in sentence rhythm; additions of a colorful, often folksy nature; and certain changes that bring the language closer to Grimmelshausen's own personal (though less standard) usage. Another revealing example is the passage in *Simplicissimus* (Book II, Ch. 8) in which Simplicius discourses on examples of prodigious memories, all taken from Colerus, but recast into a dialogue that is a masterpiece of stylistic sensitivity.[32] The goal of these adaptations appears to be total assimilation into the context, which was usually achieved.

CHAPTER 3

The Masterpiece:
The Adventurous Simplicissimus

I *Autobiography and Fiction*

THE major autobiographical elements in *Simplicissimus*, described in Chapter 1, are: Grimmelshausen's eyewitness accounts of the Imperial attack and plundering of the Wetterau, especially the atrocities committed by the Croatians; the flight of military and civilian persons, including some from Gelnhausen, to the fortress of Hanau; the siege of Magdeburg; the Westphalian campaign under General Goetz; and several events in the Upper Rhine campaign. Even within these episodes, however, the chronology is frequently altered. Certain scenes are endowed with a breath of life that presumably could come only from personal experience. Such an assumption must now be considered naive, and one to which nineteenth-century scholars, who overemphasized biography, were susceptible. Two cases in point are the battle of Wittstock (Book II, Ch. 27) and Simplicius' stay in the forest with his hermit father. As Könnecke shows, the grim "realism" of the bloody Wittstock episode was *not* based on personal experience, but was created out of a combination of printed historical sources and the novelist's own imagination (see p. 21 f.). The poignant and vivid scenes in the forest, in Book I, when the father meets and rears (unknowingly) his own son are probably based mainly on Grimmelshausen's reading of saints' legends.[1]

Even the heavily autobiographical Book I has several sheer inventions among its major episodes. There is no biographical evidence indicating the unlikely suppositions that Grimmelshausen ever had experiences closely resembling those of the hero as a simple peasant boy, or as a sylvan hermit. The Hanau episodes, insofar as they are derived from real life, probably have

[47]

a heavy overlay of experiences from Grimmelshausen's Offenburg period as a garrison soldier, but their chronology violates historical fact.[2] Book I also contains the obviously imaginary "Tree of Society" dream, the first of a series of fantastic episodes—the remaining ones being the witches' dance and the Westphalian "Paradise" of Book II, and the Mummelsee episode of Book V.

Finally, it should be noted that the novel becomes progressively less autobiographical. Books I and II reflect Grimmelshausen's life much more closely than the others. Books III through V, on the other hand, have been shown to consist mainly of inventions and literary derivations. These include all the principal segments: the "Huntsman of Soest" adventures; the captivity and marriage in Lippstadt; the stay in Paris as a physician's assistant, actor-singer, and male prostitute; the second marriage, and life as a farmer and rural philosopher; and the fantastic adventures in Book V at the Mummelsee and as a world traveller.[3] Books III through V contain only minor biographical details.

This separation of biographical fact from fiction has two purposes. First, it points up some basic errors in earlier Grimmelshausen scholarship—mainly assumptions derived from the hypothesis that Grimmelshausen actually experienced everything but the obviously fantastic events of the novel. Secondly, the overwhelming fictitious nature of the work strongly suggests that it was formed from materials, and composed according to structures other than those of his own life.

A simple and obvious principle of order in *Simplicissimus* can be extracted readily by surveying the totality of its five books. This number immediately suggests a structure related to that of the traditional five-act drama, particularly in the emphasis on the central third act, in which high points, turning points, or some other focal points are often present.[4] Book III of the novel definitely bears such emphasis: here Simplicius reaches the height of his glory as a soldier, lover, and man of wealth and social standing. There is also a sharp turning point when he is captured by the enemy near the midpoint of the Book, becomes a civilian, and marries. Another high point, though of a different nature, is constituted by Jupiter's Utopian vision of future peace and harmony in Europe in Chapters 3 through 6—an idealistic section that stands in ironical juxtaposition with Simplicius' ques-

tionable "glory." Finally, the treasure discovered near the midpoint of Book III provides a concrete focal symbol for the ambiguous "apex" of his career.

Book III, then, contains a complex kind of peripetia. We can,
therefore, expect Books I and II to "rise" toward this center, and
IV and V to "fall off" from it. That this is at least a partially
correct description becomes apparent when one considers, on the
purely sociological level, the hero's gradual elevation in society
from a crude peasant to a schooled but inexperienced youth, to
a jester, soldier, and noncommissioned officer, then to the status
of a gallant gentleman. Then, in Book IV, the process of social
degradation is marked in the sequence of professions constituted by physician's assistant, actor-singer, male prostitute, quack,
and common soldier. This thesis must be qualified, however,
by the recognition of his definite elevation in Book V, as gentleman farmer, scholar, and later in Russia, as an accomplished
and respected engineer. On the other hand, he is still declining
in a psychological and moral sense.

The above overall development in a rough graphic diagram
would show a flat-topped pyramid, with the upper third representing Book III. Descending down the sides, the middle halves
of the two slopes would be Books II and IV, and the bottom
sections I and V.[5] This is a useful diagram not only because it
graphically shows the crucial midpoint (or better: *midsection*)
of the novel, but also because it suggests parallels along the two
sides of the figure. Outstanding in this respect are the beginning
and the end: at both points, Simplicius is a hermit, living by
himself in the forest. Also, near the midpoint of both Books I
and V, we encounter visionary episodes (the "Tree of Society"
and the Mummelsee, resp.), both several chapters long, and both
providing Simplicius with a total view of the world, each from
a different vantage point. These two visions are actually parts of
a triad completed by the Jupiter episode in Book III. Thus,
returning to the image of the pyramid, we find these three
points in I, III, and V in strikingly symmetrical relationship
with one another. Finally, we can readily find parallels between
Books II and IV, for in both—and near the midpoints—Satanic
forces reach maximum strength. Book II is centered on the
witches' dance, connected with Simplicius' entry into the war as
a combatant, and foreshadowing increasingly frequent devil

motifs. Book IV is centered on Simplicius' adventures as a "free-booter," and his encounter with Olivier, the most fearsomely evil character of the book. There is also a meaningful progression in these two books with respect to Satanic influences in the life of the hero. In Book II, Simplicius is enticed into the devil's worldly temptations. It is as if the witches' dance had cast a spell over him. In Book IV, Simplicius fights first an inconclusive wrestling match, then a battle of conscience with Olivier, a veritable devil in the flesh. The good principle triumphs when Simplicius is removed from this influence by Olivier's sudden death. Thus the midpoint of Book II signals Simplicius' *entrance* into a Satanic world of temptation; that of Book IV his eventual *exit* from it.

The skeletal plot of the five books, as sketched in pyramid form, reveals one single principle of plot organization—the sharp accentuation of midpoints.[6] As will be seen, such emphasis exists in most of Grimmelshausen's writings. Midpoint analysis, however, yields little more than pivotal points and interconnections. These are important matters, but there are far richer, more complex, and more interesting aspects to the composition of this novel.

The influence of the picaresque, or rogue's novel on *Simplicissimus* was touched upon in Chapter 2. As we have seen, during the conception of the novel, Grimmelshausen did not have the standard Spanish works of this genre (*Lazarillo de Tormes, Guzmán de Alfarache, Rinconete y cortadillo*) uppermost in his mind, but rather Charles Sorel's atypical novel in French, derived only in part from Spanish predecessors. Thus it is immediately suggested that the standard figure of the *pícaro*, though by no means irrelevant to Simplicissimus is not among his closest kin.

The main character of the picaresque novel is generally a young man of the lower classes, whose story consists of a series of adventures as a servant or subordinate, and who passes from one master to another. He tells his own story and encounters a variety of character types and social stations, which are seen from the underdog's or "worm's eye" point of view, thus providing an opportunity for criticism and satire of the leaders of society. Considerable entertainment value is afforded by clever ruses and adventurous scrapes. Individual anecdotes about them are told almost as independent tales. Thus the plot is loosely organized. The hero does not develop under the impact of his experiences, but remains the same "rogue" throughout. Amorality and opportunism pervade the atmosphere, and some guarded anticlerical sentiments and secretly anti-Christian views are occasionally revealed between the lines.

That Simplicissimus is a "rogue" can scarcely be denied, and the many features that Grimmelshausen's novel has in common with the picaresque are obvious. Simplicius begins his life in a low station, and at a near-bestial stage of existence. Up to a point, he, too, views most of human society from below, especially in Books I, II, and IV. Much of Simplicius' tale concerns a series of servitudes under successive masters. At one point (the end of Chapter 28 in Book II) he even shows that he has kept a mental record of their number, when he notes that the dragoon is his sixth master. A few episodes are centered on typically roguish ruses possessing much entertainment value. This is especially true of the theft of the pastor's bacon at the end of Book II, the appropriation of the landlord's rabbit at the end of Book III, and the calf's eye episode in Book I, Chapter 29.

Frequently, however, Simplicius is only in part a picaro, and at still other times, the world of the Spanish picaresque novel is completely foreign to him. The high point of the novel, as already described, clearly removes the work from the picaresque world, for here Simplicius' manner is largely that of a nobleman. There is even an antipicaresque role-reversal when one clearly identifiable picaro, Springinsfeld, becomes his subordinate. To this must be added Simplicius' relatively exalted roles in Book V. All this is not only a matter of character and theme, but of the composition of the novel. To remain truly picaresque, the tale must move in adventurous waves, in ups and downs of fortune that are more or less equal in their crests and valleys, lest the hero rise too high for his lower-class origins or fall too low for his essential self-esteem and autonomy. The picaro must thus remain static in character—something that is clearly not true of Simplicius. After all, the novel tells of a character who grows from childhood into early manhood.

Above all, Simplicius is *not* presented as a lower-class character, for on the very title page he is expressly identified as "Melchior Sternfels von Fuchshaim," who was only *raised* as a peasant. In a sense, then, his picaresque qualities are illusory, a trick of fate obscuring his "real" nature, which, according to the values of the time, depended on lineage and legal birthrights. Simplicius eventually had to behave as a nobleman, for noble blood coursed through his veins. This whole issue becomes a matter of literary forms upon consideration of the role that his nobility plays in the structure of the novel; for as in the aristocratic novel of the time, we have in *Simplicissimus* an anagnorisis or "recognition scene" (with the "knan" in Book V, Ch. 8) in which his noble lineage is revealed. Of course an immediate qualification must be made here: in the chapters surrounding the revelation, Simplicius behaves more like a peasant than he has since Book I. A bitter irony attends his "nobility" as a result of this juxtaposition, as at so many other points when fortune momentarily smiles on him. Conversely, his career as a farmer turns sour, and the other side of his social being likewise remains unfulfilled.

The conclusion to be drawn from this combination of the highborn and the lowborn in Simplicius' life, and of the corresponding literary forms of the picaresque and gallant novel in his story, is much the same as that reached about Grimmelshausen himself: there is a prevailing, painful sociological ambivalence at the core of this novelistic figure. This factor in particular, however, greatly contributes to his breadth of experience and his interestingly problematic qualities.

II *Character: Its Development and Masks*

The term "Bildungsroman" has been used frequently to classify *Simplicissimus,* although nearly always with reservations.[7] In Chapter 2 (p. 41 ff.), it was suggested that the novel has definite connections with this most German of narrative forms if broadly defined. As such it is indeed a milestone in the history of those German novels telling the story of a boy who becomes a man. The question, then, is whether much is made of this fact in the composition of the novel. Also to be asked is the question of whether an organic principle of character growth determines the sequence of the hero's experiences, as would be required by a stricter definition of the genre of which the model and standard is Goethe's *Wilhelm Meister*.

The point in the novel most clearly germane to this problem is Chapter 9 of Book I, when Simplicius' *Bildung*—or combination of formal education and character formation—begins. It consists of the Christian education and upbringing provided by the hermit. The title of this chapter is "Simplicius is transformed from a Beast into a Christian human being," which carries the implication that Christianization is tantamount to humanization. This is the first major step in Simplicius' character development. The narrator refers to his earlier self also in terms of "the tablet of my heart, which was as soft as wax and still bare." There follows a summary of the main articles of Christian indoctrination, which Simplicius fervently absorbs within a mere three-week period. Then the Aristotelian idea of the *tabula rasa,* or blank slate of the untrained mind, is expounded, with learned references. The aim of this "writing" process—the perfection of the soul—is repeatedly emphasized.

It would be absurd to attribute a "perfect soul" to Simplicius at any stage of this story. Apparently, Grimmelshausen loosely identified the above process with Christianization. In any case, a giant step has been taken here, in that a full-fledged human being is created out of the near-animal that he has been. It is thus no accident that, as soon as the process is completed, the most important sign of identity—his name—is bestowed on him. Juxtaposed with this is the instruction in precisely what human beings are, and in the fundamental relationship between father, mother, and child. The remainder of his training in the next two years consists of learning to read and write, and to accomplish the essential daily tasks for survival in the forest. These matters, however, are passed over almost summarily, as if they were little more than elaborations on the fundamentals learned during the first three weeks.

In spite of Simplicius' elevation to genuinely human stature, he is not prepared for integration into human society. When, at the end of Chapter II, he announces the completion of his *Bildung,* in the same breath he points out his simplemindedness in dealings with people. The socializing process is no doubt in his father's mind when, about to die, he admonishes the son to follow the three tenets: know thyself, avoid bad company, and remain steadfast. In these few episodes there is a focus on maturation of character, as in the totality of a *Bildungsroman.* There is, however, nothing comparable to the organic unfolding process as presented in the Goethean form of this genre. We must also consider whether in *Simplicissimus* the purpose of *Bildung* is integration into society, as it is with Goethe.

The stage following that of Simplicius' two years in the forest consists primarily of a direct and merciless confrontation with the life of the times. It becomes immediately apparent that the above-mentioned self-characterization is true: he is, in society, *ein reiner Tor*, or "innocent fool"—a term used to describe Parzival as a child. Simplicius' purely Christian upbringing is put to the test by Society, as represented in Hanau, whose moralizing, but naive chastizer he becomes until the inevitable crisis occurs at the transition from Book I to Book II, resulting from his boorish behavior with a noble lady at a ball. His imprisonment in a goose-pen and the subsequent attempt by Ramsay to drive him insane—to make a new kind of "fool" out of him—put an end to his role as "reiner Tor."

There follows a second stage of development. Ramsay's plot leads not to madness, but to a highly sharpened mind in his nephew, who is now better able to survive in society and yet—to a degree—to remain honest as a Christian in a world hostile to the pious. No longer the innocent fool, he is now a sly buffoon, a *Schalksnarr*. There is something of a major psychological development in the transition, involving not only self-knowledge, but knowledge of the self's relations with others. Not to be overlooked, however, is the considerable psychological implausibility inherent in his roles as fool. Simplicius demonstrates a sophisticated kind of knowledge which he could not possibly possess when he calls a foppishly-dressed and long-haired officer a "hermaphrodite" (Book I, Ch. 19); and when he glibly sermonizes on adultery (Book I, Ch. 21).[8] He thereupon returns to his former naiveté for several chapters. The highest degree of his social awareness is reached in Book II, after his transformation into a "calf." It can be plausibly argued (as does Alt) that the woodenly moralizing Simplicius of Book I is a vestige of a previous version of the novel, resembling the earlier sections of the *Satirical Pilgrim*, in its abstract moralizations and its total lack of action and esprit. Granting this to be possible, however, the overall course of Books I and II, as described above, remains the same, especially with respect to Simplicius' transformation into a buffoon.

One aspect of this transition can scarcely be overemphasized.

The direction that has been set for most of the remainder of the novel is *away from* organic, inward character-development. Simplicius' survival depends on externalities. As a fool, he is called upon (as he is repeatedly later on) to don a mask and play the role imposed by it. Much of what follows, then, is *not* essentially the story of a boy becoming a man, for he is now full-grown in the terms of the author: his soul has been written on, and he knows how to survive in society.

There is one final and definite stage of psychological transformation near the end of the novel. In Book V, Chapter 23, the hero, while reading, encounters a reference to the Delphic oracle commanding "Know Thyself." Upon surveying his past life, he arrives at a self-knowledge which—at least for the unit of Books I through V—is stated with finality. For there follows a typically Baroque cataloguing of his past experiences which he now characterizes only in the most negative terms: vain, unsubstantial, transitory, sinful, and corrupt. "All is vanity." He then bids a lengthy "Adieu, World!" to life in society and returns to the forest, having been granted—so he thinks at the time—full and everlasting enlightenment.

In determining to what extent the novel is a *Bildungsroman,* one should consider the fact that the hero has indeed been subjected to a course of events leading to a definite relationship with the world.[9] We may further agree on the point that it is— to say the least—a *negative* relationship. This should not, however, make any essential difference in the *structure* of the novel as *Bildungsroman*; it does, however, make the work exceptional in its *theme*. Whether this is legitimate for a *Bildungsroman* (or anti-*Bildungsroman*), by narrower definition, is a moot question. At least in the matter of psychological development—both as individual and as collective being—Simplicius does undergo a process essential to the genre. Yet there is as much in the development of the action that is irrelevant to this process. One may argue that a novel can and often does combine features of many types of the genre, and should be analyzed as such. This approach is inevitable with such a many-faceted and multi-levelled work as *Simplicissimus*. In view of the relative insignificance of *Bildung* throughout large segments of the novel, however, it is surely an exaggeration to conclude that the book is *best* described as being *essentially* a Baroque *Bildungsroman*.

We must, then, look further for concepts that may perhaps fully embrace this generically elusive work of fiction.

As indicated above, there are processes of "character development" in *Simplicissimus* which are not essential to the *Bildungsroman*. These evolve primarily out of "role-playing." The sequence of roles extends from the beginning of Book II to the final episode—between the second and third steps of the previously outlined psychological development. This constitutes one of the most elaborate sets of strands in the fabric of the work, and requires detailed analysis.

That Grimmelshausen intended us to view Simplicius as an actor on the stage of the *theatrum mundi* is most dramatically shown by the many changes of his garb or "costume." The first such external transformation is unmistakably emphasized, so that we should be all the more sensitive to the subsequent ones. This occurs near the beginning of the Hanau section in Book I, Chapter 21, where Simplicius is thoroughly washed and groomed by Ramsay's servants, then bedecked with finery far above his station, and "mylord Simplicius sat there like a young baron," as the narrator informs us ironically. The artificiality of this process of costume-changing has, shortly before, been indicated by the application of cosmetics to highlight his crude and wild features as a forest creature, so that a life-size portrait of him could be painted in his "original" state before he is recostumed. When he dons his new garb, it is so lavish and has such colorful detail that we cannot help but visualize a second portraitlike image. Thus by cleverly inducing the reader to see two pictures side-by-side, Grimmelshausen has vividly portrayed his character in a moment of sharp transition. Simplicius is now called upon to conform to his new surroundings, and a conflict inevitably ensues, for he is as yet unaware that he is not only called upon to put on a mask, but also to act out the part. Thus the second half of Book I is centered mainly on a crudely comical figure (with the above-mentioned exceptions in Chapters 19 and 21), having a pure soul but being totally inept in dealing with the environment for which his costume is designed.

The major psychological development leading him into the next stage of buffoon has been dealt with above in connection with the *Bildungsroman*. To be noted additionally is, first, the extremity of the measures needed to accomplish the transformation—his trips to Heaven and Hell in Chapters 5 and 6 of Book II. Secondly, a revealing commentary is made on the nature of this and all subsequent play-acting soon after Simplicius has become a calf. This occurs in Chapter Eight, in a conversation with the pastor, the only person fully aware of Simplicius' dissemblance. When the boy expresses concern over the sinfulness of deception, the pastor reassures him: "You needn't concern yourself about that. The foolish world wants to be deceived; and since your senses have been left intact, use them to your advantage." There follows the extremely important advice: "Imagine that you are like unto a *Phoenix,* that you have passed through fire from a state of stupidity to one of understanding, and thus have been reborn to a new way of human life."

The perceptive reader of the novel may here recall another Phoenix figure—that depicted on the frontispiece, with the verses below it beginning "I was born through fire, like the Phoenix. . . ." Implicit in the frontispiece, and its motto, is a commentary on the role-sequence. The verse describes, above all, Simplicius' Phoenixlike progression of changes as an all-inclusive journey. He passes not only through fire, but also through the air, the water, and over land—thus indicating the all-embracing four "elements" and, therewith, the whole cosmos. The parts of the creature's body—the fish's tail, the wings, the webbed foot of a duck, a horse's hoof—are designed to point to all elements except fire, which receives sufficient emphasis in the opening lines of the verse. The pictures in the book held by the figure suggest, by the variety of significant objects related to several episodes, that the whole book is symbolized. Above all, a number of actors' masks are strewn about the floor. Grimmelshausen could scarcely have pointed more emphatically to the artificial and insubstantial nature of Simplicius' many postures and faces.

This is not character development or unfolding as commonly understood, for at least as much is *concealed* by the process as is *revealed.* From the beginning of Book II onward, then, we can expect a series of fleeting, externalized scenes, which would have little relevance to character, were it not for the frequent comments of the hermit narrator, an older and wiser man who provides a stable element of character. With his critical and satirical comments on Simplicius' vanity and folly in the various roles, he unifies everything with the unchanging Christian point of view that had been implanted by his father in Book I.[10]

Simplicius' role as fool in Book I is changed in Book II by a meaningful set of reversals. In the second half of Book I, he is dressed as a nobleman, but in society he behaves like the crudest of peasants, at times even like an animal. Then in Book II, he wears a calf's skin and the ears of an ass, but his behavior, as revealed to the reader along with his thoughts, is supremely civilized and sophisticated. The real louts and animals in human form turn to be society's leaders:

More piggish than swine, more ferocious than lions, more lewd than he-goats, more envious than dogs, more uncontrollable than horses, cruder than asses, more drunk than cattle, slyer than foxes, more gluttonous than wolves, more foolish than monkeys, and more poisonous than snakes and toads. (Book II, Ch. 7)

Furthermore, animality is woven into the fabric of Book II with many more such analogies and metaphors. All this, combined with Simplicius' clever buffoonery, amounts to an ingenious, often ambiguous, interplay of reality and appearances. Simplicius, though externally in servitude, reigns inwardly supreme over his masters.

The hero's abrupt loss of his position as jester comes about near the midpoint (Chapter 14) of Book II when his harsh servitude under the Croatians begins. This sudden transition precipitates a series of brief but meaningful roles leading to his becoming a full-fledged soldier. With the barbaric Colonel Corpes, commander of the Croatians, Simplicius remains a "fool," but is degraded by beatings and menial tasks. A meaningful bit of play-acting occurs when he is forced, by his sadistic masters, to act like a dog under the table. That he is now a totally different kind of fool is further indicated by a change of garb, the main difference from the previous one being the longer donkey-ears. Aside from suggesting even greater folly in the future than he has already committed (such as endangering himself by his overly frank satire), this sign of his role takes on two further associations anticipating later events. First, the ears link him with the Satanic when they are mistaken for devil's horns by a soldier, thus causing Simplicius to act like a devil to frighten him away (Ch. 16). Secondly, they become the repository for the money that he finds, after he has cut them off and converted them into armbands functioning as money-belts. Thus, money and the devil are intimately connected.

There follows the eerie witch episode. No perceptible change, internal or external, takes place in his role at the time, for he is an unwilling and passive observer of the witches' flight through the air and their dance. Yet a stigma is put on him, and from this point into the beginning of Book V, the devil's almost constant presence is suggested by a great variety of figures, motifs, and verbal images. These are, however, primarily external matters. Only at two points does Simplicius himself really play the role of a devil. This occurs first at the above-mentioned occasion in Chapter 16, which is unpremeditated and temporary, and is designed merely to frighten away his captors. And he is mistaken for the devil again in the final chapter of Book II—into which much comedy is injected. And so much of Simplicius' guilt for stealing the parson's bacon is mitigated by his later paying for it that Simplicius can hardly be characterized as Satanic. He merely has a long series of close brushes with the devil, who neither enters into Simplicius' character, nor seriously into his roles. The devil's sulphuric aura does pervade the atmosphere, and occasionally, as will be seen, enters into of other characters (Springinsfeld and, above all, Olivier). The source of it all is the witchery of this central episode of Book II.[11]

Simplicius remains in his fool's habit (with cropped ears) for a brief period when he joins the Imperial forces besieging Magdeburg. His attire is only slightly altered in Chapter 19 when it is adorned with ribbons. (Again, as in Chapter 21 of Book II, he is approaching a role for which finery is appropriate.) His desire to escape the confines of his fool's appearance becomes so great, however, that he seizes the first opportunity to don a new garb—a woman's dress. This bawdily comical interlude, during which he is an ardently pursued maidservant (Ch. 25), is sandwiched between two serious stages on his way to becoming a soldier.

Previously he has been introduced to two pairs of persons who ultimately form a meaningful allegory of Simplicius' moral conflicts. Hertzbruder the Elder and the Younger assume the function of virtuous advisors, previously performed by the hermit, then by the pastor at Hanau. Their Satanic counterparts—the Provost and Olivier—act as their foils. Once both the older members of the two pairs die, Simplicius is left as the object of contention between Hertzbruder and Olivier—an angel and a devil competing for the possession of a soul. In the pattern of good and evil in which Simplicius is involved, the right path is apparently to remain a fool for the time being, or at least not to become further involved in the war than he already is. This is made clear by both the Hanau pastor's and the elder Hertzbruder's prediction that removing the fool's garb would spell danger for him. Olivier prevails in the first stage of the battle, for Hertzbruder the younger must leave after being falsely accused of theft. The elder Hertzbruder then dies, Olivier (with the ominous Provost in the background) is left as the dominant force. It is under Olivier's aegis that Simplicius goes foraging, falls into the absurd role of maid, and then finds himself, when his true sex is discovered, under suspicion of spying and in imminent danger of torture and execution.

The bloody battle of Wittstock intervenes in the case against Simplicius. He is, significantly, rescued by his guardian angel, Hertzbruder, who evens the scale of good and evil by killing the formidable Provost. Now the way is clear for Simplicius to take the next step toward a military career. He becomes the orderly of a Swedish officer. In this capacity, Simplicius' prowess as a soldier is demonstrated by his strategy in combatting the lice under the cuirass that he is required to wear by his commander (Ch. 28). As it turns out, he will fight other battles almost as trivial, in spite of his promotions after his recapture by Imperial forces.

His new master, a dragoon, is a penurious lout, yet Simplicius manages to rise to hitherto unknown heights during this brief tour of duty in Book II, Chapter 29, ending with his full acceptance into the military as a dragoon. This transition is emphatically signaled by a new and elegant uniform, purchased with booty acquired during the stay at "Paradise." He now cuts a handsome figure, and pursues this new fortune further by learning the ennobling arts of fencing and hunting. The death of his master is a stroke of fortune in that he acquires thereby a legacy of money, clothing, a horse, and a new position. In the same way as when he arrived at Hanau, he is dramatically transformed into a new figure, primarily with a new costume and all that it means. His only just claim to prowess as a soldier, however, rests on the battle of the lice and a few foraging expeditions. A new name caps the fiction: the Huntsman of Soest, suggested by his green garb resembling that of a hunter. Along with the acquisition of further wealth and property, Simplicius is now in a position to command two man servants (instead of a mere orderly), in spite of his lack of appropriate rank. As he narrates the tale, the older Simplicius interjects unmistakable gibes at this folly, culminating in an outright condemnation of the Huntsman's sin of pride, near the end of Chapter 30.

One of his first notable deeds as Huntsman, however, mitigates his guilt. This occurs as part of the farcical tale of the theft of the bread and bacon, in Chapter 31. Simplicius, it is true, plays the devil here, but the comedy and triviality of the whole episode make it impossible to condemn him. In fact, his picaresque cleverness is designed to be admirable. Furthermore, this German Robin Hood afterwards makes more than adequate payment for the stolen goods. The sum total of this adventure, however, is scarcely of more consequence than the battle of the lice and hardly worthy of a man sporting such attire and enjoying, supposedly, such widespread acclaim as a military leader —in command of half a dozen soldiers!

More serious wrongdoing is approached in Chapter 1 of Book III, when Simplicius invents several clever ruses designed to deceive the enemy, but brings suspicion of witchcraft upon himself. In Chapter 2 he prepares devil masks to frighten his foes. This impending change of costume is impeded, however, by the reports of the Huntsman of Werl (later revealed to be Olivier), who is committing atrocities in the name of the more virtuous Huntsman. Simplicius' rage is aptly expressed by his stageworthy *auto da fé* of chopping up his green huntsman's costume and burning it (Ch. 2). When, however, he captures and humiliates his rival, an ambiguous state of affairs arises with respect to Simplicius' affiliation with Satan. The allegorical defeat of the Devil in the form of Olivier is accomplished with the aid of two other "devils" (Simplicius' servants in disguise)—possible evidence for the practice of witchcraft. Simplicius himself does not, however, don the devil's costume. Above all, the upshot of the Huntsman of Werl affair is an increase in his generosity and virtue. But there remains a sharp difference between the reality and the appearance of his activities. Though unintentionally, he now produces illusions, i.e., works of the devil. The control over his own fate increasingly eludes him, in spite of his apparent power and glory. To be further considered is the increased hostility of the persons in his immediate environment. Thus Simplicius, in his role of the Huntsman, is complex and ambiguous indeed, and considerable qualification must be made with regard to the "height of glory" that may all too simplistically be bestowed on him by the pyramidal diagram of the plot.

The Great God Jupiter, the madman who now precipitately enters the scene, serves to underscore the true nature of Simplicius' "heroism." This quixotic "wise fool," caught up in pipe dreams of a glorious future, describes a great German Hero who will enforce the universal peace, harmony, and order for which Europe is yearning. Irony pervades the passage, not only because Jupiter is obviously mad, but also because of the situation in which his Utopia is portrayed: an ambush of a convoy—an activity that, to say the least, is far removed from that of a virtuous *miles christianus* fighting for a just cause. Simplicius' "heroism" is thus further undermined by this juxtaposition of reality and ideality. Furthermore, Simplicius is subtly shown to be untrue to himself (as he was revealed in his frank utterances as a fool at Hanau) by transferring all his erstwhile "foolishness" to Jupiter—an action subsequently symbolized by Jupiter's becoming Simplicius' "fool" and advisor. He draws parallels between the madman and his former self:

I thought to myself, that the fellow might perhaps not be the fool that he pretended to be, but rather was cooking up recipes such as those that I prepared in Hanau, in order to manage better an escape from us. . . . (Ch. 6)

And he later says:

. . . so strange is fortune, and so changeable is time! A short time ago, the lice were plaguing *me*, and now I have the Flea-God in my power; half a year ago, I served a simple dragoon as servant-boy; now I was master of two manservants, who called me 'Sir.' . . . (Ch. 8)

Irony is compounded here by self-irony, for in pointing out the parallel between his own battle with the lice and Jupiter's with fleas (Book II, Ch. 28 and Book III, Ch. 6, resp.) he suggests a relationship between his own triviality and impotence as a soldier, and Jupiter's inability to become the savior of the world.

Simplicius' megalomania is expressed, in well-known traditional terms, as a variety of the sin of pride to which is added a strong element of folly. The hermit-narrator interjects such comments as the following: "My pride increased with my fortune. . . . In the most senseless folly that ever a reasonable man has committed, everone hoped to maintain the upper hand . . ." (Ch. 9); and "in sum, the most intelligent people must have considered me, without doubt, to be a young fop, whose pride necessarily would not last long, because it rested on a poor foundation, and had to be maintained by uncertain booty . . ." (Ch. 12). He plays the role well enough to be taken by some, at least, for a young nobleman (Ch. 9), and is egged on to dress in his most flamboyant costumes (Ch. 11); he even considers attempting to obtain a patent of nobility (Ch. 13). A high point of his "nobility" is reached when he becomes wealthy upon the discovery of the buried treasure (Ch. 12). Counterpointing this, however, is the eerie atmosphere of the haunted house in which he finds it, as well as Jupiter's advice to rid himself of this root of all evil, particularly because of the envy surrounding him—which threatens his very life. Only a stroke of fortune— his capture by the enemy—wrests him from this peril. Ironically, this occurs immediately after he has resolved henceforth to feign humility, to dress less ostentatiously, and to purchase friendship with some of his wealth.

The Lippstadt episode takes up most of the second half of Book III. Just as Simplicius' folly in war dominates the first half, so does his folly in love dominate the second, as is underscored by the narrator's continuation of his self-reproaches. The manifestations of his sin of pride continue, compounded by amorous gallantries and associated activities, such as the reading of love stories, further musical training, and the consolidation of his fortune. Flamboyance in dress is continued, even to the extent of decking out his own page-boy like a peacock (Ch. 17). The pretense of his nobility is likewise continued, particularly when he nearly obtains an officer's candidacy. His eminent success as a lover is proven by his fathering of six children, almost simultaneously, by six burgher girls. To cap these conquests, he acquires a wife—albeit by means of the uproariously comical

shotgun wedding in bed. The seemingly unfortunate young lecher
is thus converted overnight into an unexpectedly loving and re-
spectful husband—a role that he assumes easily, though it lasts
only a week.

The brevity of the marriage is not the only qualifying factor
in his career as a husband. There is, above all, the aforementioned group of six girls, recently seduced by him. Thus he
must play-act as husband to the extent that his past love-life
is suppressed and not allowed to be revealed at a church wedding. Furthermore, his position with respect to the church is
shown to be ambiguous and perilous to his soul, when he and a
clergyman debate the matter of love, and Simplicius simply lies
his way out of the situation (Ch. 19 and 20). The clergyman
nonetheless has sounded a warning note, thus serving the same
purpose as the pastor at Hanau, and later Jupiter. The hero is
still, as in the first half of Book III, at the same ambiguous
"height" of his fortune, as he expressly states at the opening of
Chapters 16 and 19. In the latter passage, however, there is a
warning of an imminent fall. As counterweights to his gallant
"nobility," periodic references to his humble upbringing appear
like leitmotifs. In Chapter 17 there is a vivid reminder, by the
Prophetess of Soest, of the "Knan," when she enigmatically
prophesies the latter's leading on a leash the daughter of Simplicius' "wet-nurse" (who happens to have been a goat). Furthermore, Simplicius expresses compunctions at entering the "high
society" of Lippstadt, for it was "no place for a fellow of such
humble origin as that which, as I was aware, was mine." Referring to his wife-to-be, he says of himself "when you consider
your origin, you are scarcely worthy of sitting where she places
her shoes." Such thoughts are appropriately juxtaposed with the
precarious situation of his wealth—which takes him to Cologne.
On his journey, the motifs associated with his humble origin
continue to crop up. Simplicius encounters a farmer and his son
and overhears them in an exchange of profanities and obscenities.
This follows, with definite irony, on the heels of a chapter in
which the opportunity of becoming an officer's candidate seems
to be in the offing.

The Cologne episode places Simplicius in a totally different
role from that of Lippstadt. He becomes again the roguish
prankster, and shines in some of his former picaresque glory by

means of the sly ruse of obtaining a hare for himself and his fellow boarders, in order to eat well for once at the table of the stingy landlord. Thus for the third consecutive time, a book of the novel ends with Simplicius' appropriation of a delicacy with the help of clever picaresque tactics. This is Grimmelshausen's most purposeful use of the stock figure of the picaro: in all three cases, he provides a comical interlude between two serious roles.

A change in costume in Chapter 1 of Book IV clearly dramatizes his next role as Dr. Canard's assistant. Here he dons the cast-off clothing of a nobleman who has purchased finery in the new style for his Paris adventures. The threadbare image of nobility that he projects is a fitting one for the association with Canard, a stereotype figure of the nouveau riche, and of a physician who cynically exploits his medical skills among wealthy nobles, and is even a panderer on the side.

Simplicius' prestige seems to be on the rise when he becomes the "Beau Alman" (as Grimmelshausen calls him) of the Paris stage and bedchambers. At this point, the previously discussed pyramidal structure is especially inadequate, for it cannot indicate the extreme ambiguity of the part he performs in Paris. In a new way, his adventures in France represent simultaneously a high and a low, both unmatched by any other segment of the novel. Here he becomes an actor in the literal sense, costumed, made-up, and acting out a part in the theater. Externally he cuts the most splendid figure of the novel, even enhancing it with singing and lute-playing. He is fawned over as never before. But nowhere else does he sink to such a low of self-abasement in his accompanying role of male prostitute. His guilt is slightly mitigated by the fact that he has been tricked into it (having been secretly administered an aphrodisiac by Canard), and also because he is feigning passion in these bedroom scenes. The sum total of the Paris experiences is a perversion of his role as lover in the second half of Book III, where he at least has had the saving grace of robustness in his sex-life (fathering seven children), and in his brief but genuine marital bliss before his departure for Cologne. Mockery is made of these experiences by the translation of his genuine yearning for his wife into a pompous stage version of the Orpheus and Eurydice legend, and by engaging in meaningless sexual adventures. Drained of manhood, and weary of the game, he is ripe for a radical transformation, which comes about through a disfiguring case of smallpox contracted after the departure from Paris.

Deprived of his finery and wealth, his handsome features marred with pockmarks, contorted eyes, and ugly stubble of hair, he has obviously been costumed and made-up for a new role. Even his singing voice, a gift to Venus' favorites, is silenced. The gallant warrior and lover of Book III is now a pitifully degraded creature, who must take recourse to his wits in order to survive. In the role he now assumes—that of a quack—he is both dishonest and dishonorable. He achieves some success, even acquires the popular title of "doctor," but his repulsive outward appearance and loss in prestige surely convey a significant amount of irony.

The next step downward occurs when Simplicius is suddenly whisked away by soldiers of the Phillipsburg garrison, and again he dons a soldier's costume, this time with a musket on his shoulder—the foot soldier occupying the lowest prestige position in the military. Concerning this descent, he remarks: "Then I recommenced the life I had led in Soest, except that I was not permitted to lead and command parties" (Book IV, Ch. 9). Added to poverty and hunger is the contempt of his fellows. Now his picaro role—the amusingly roguish one—finds a variation in that of an outright scoundrel. At least he projects such an image in his garrison. In this situation, his peril involves twofold variation—physical (Ch. 10), and spiritual (Ch. 11). Being almost drowned in the Rhine is thus a parallel to the danger he incurs in a religious sense. This juxtaposition is ironical insofar as Simplicius cries out for God's help when about to drown, but when safe, defies the clergyman's remonstrances, which, though unsuccessful, anticipate Simplicius' subsequent pilgrimage and conversion.

In the episode following the conversation with the pastor (Ch. 12), Hertzbruder—who by now must be recognized as Simplicius' guardian angel—opportunely descends and relieves his friend's misery. There is a change of costume to that of cavalryman, whereby Simplicius' status is slightly raised, and again he is on the verge of further elevation to officer. A sudden twist in the course of events then perverts Hertzbruder's intentions. Instead of continuing on the path of the *miles christianus*, of which

Hertzbruder is an idealized example, Simplicius becomes a "Merodebruder," a worthless, parasitic type of soldier who engages mainly in ambush and plunder. A further descent, in a moral sense, comes about when he joins Olivier and temporarily becomes his companion in the very worst forms of such activities.

This role is introduced by a wrestling match, ending in a draw between Simplicius and Olivier (Ch. 14), before they recognize each other. As in Book II, we have a number of sections alternating between Olivier and Hertzbruder, indicating vacillation between an evil and a good principle. This time, however, it is an arduous battle, almost to the death, suggested by the initial violent confrontation, then rising to a purely allegorical level throughout the remainder of the long section (Chs. 14 through 21). The relationship is a curiously fraternal one, as underscored by Olivier's frequent reference to Simplicius as "brother." Olivier's motivation for the form of address is readily understood on the grounds that the elder Hertzbruder had predicted that Simplicius would avenge Olivier's death. On a deeper level, we can perceive a bond between them, particularly in their simultaneous "huntsman" roles at Soest and Werl. There, of course, Olivier had suffered an ignominious defeat at the hands of Simplicius, but the identity of this foe is unknown to him.

Throughout the eleven chapters devoted to Olivier, Simplicius is conspicuously passive (aside from the wrestling match). He is actually a freebooter only in a qualified sense. He wears the new clothing given him by Olivier (Ch. 16), but inwardly is engaged in a constant moral struggle against Olivier. Much of this section consists of Olivier's narration of his story—a veritable catalogue of mortal sins—to which Simplicius listens in silent horror. The height of Simplicius' amoral passivity occurs when he follows Olivier and takes part, though unwillingly, in the desecration of a church by using its tower as a look-out for the purpose of ambushing. With the appearance of a coach, however, Simplicius reverts somewhat to the Robin Hood role of Soest in his refusal to massacre the woman and children in the coach. Yet he remains with Olivier and avenges his death, as prophesied. But even when this villain is removed from the scene, the freebooter lives on briefly in Simplicius when, with murderous threats, he demands Olivier's wealth from the farmer. Simplicius is never completely possessed, yet is definitely influenced by "devils."

The pendulum swinging between the devil and the angel has, however, reversed its direction, and Book IV ends with Simplicius being again under Hertzbruder's protection, which increases throughout the early part of Book V. Rapid, often bewildering transformation is the keynote for Simplicius' roles in this last Book. Beginning as a not-so-pious pilgrim, though in appropriate garb, on the journey to Einsiedel with Hertzbruder, Simplicius shows that he is not ready for a spiritual regeneration, to say nothing of adopting Hertzbruder's saintliness. Some of Olivier's aura is still with him in the form of a devil that a priest exorcises from another man in Simplicius' presence (Book V, Ch. 2). In addition, Olivier's money is still in Simplicius' possession. Thus his conversion to Catholicism is not accompanied by a change of role.

A brief rise in Simplicius' fortunes comes about in Chapter 4, when he finally achieves the long-sought officer's commission— but along with a unit so depleted (seven soldiers and one sergeant) that he hardly merits his captaincy. Yet Simplicius is briefly cast in the role of *miles christianus*, fighting for a cause he believes to be just, and under Hertzbruder's beneficient influence. The development, beginning in Book III, toward Simplicius' becoming an officer is thus externally completed, but this tour of duty is trivial and short, and ends in total defeat. To this is added Hertzbruder's emasculation by a bullet and the mortal illness that follows.

With Simplicius' captaincy, Grimmelshausen has begun a rapid sequence of brief episodes that comprise a recapitulation of almost all the main roles Simplicius has played. Leaving Hertzbruder behind at a spa, he reassumes his responsibility as husband by making the journey to Lippstadt (Book V, Ch. 5). The detour to Cologne underscores the vanity of his now renounced soldier's life, for Jupiter delivers an impassioned denunciation of the war. Then, upon arriving in Lippstadt, the news of the death of his wife ends his illusory role as husband. Circumstances prevent his adopting the role of father to his son. Returning to the spa, he again becomes a Don Juan (Ch. 6), with overtones of the Paris adventures. Now he consorts, for the first time, with an outright prostitute, a lady claiming nobility, but "more *mobilis* than *nobilis*," and turning out to be none other than the notorious Courasche of the Simplician sequel. In the same chapter, a brief encounter with a kind of witch doctor suggests both the presence of the devil in Simplicius' activities and his ability to ward off the worst of such influences, in that the gentleman is forced to leave the scene with scratches on his face (like another "devil," Olivier). Chapter 7 places Simplicius in a position of greater social prestige, furthered by the cultivation of elegant manners and associations, and allowing himself to be addressed by the empty title of captain. This role mainly suggests that of the Huntsman of Soest. Soon, however, we find him married to a vulgar woman of the peasant class and reverting to the life-style of the beginning of the novel when he lived with his "Knan." The revelation, made in Chapter 8, that his wife is a slut and drunkard is ironically coupled with the encounter with the Knan, who relates the facts of Simplicius' noble origins. The calamitous incongruity of his situation reaches its crisis in Chapter 9. Having gained documentary proof of his noble birth, his wife makes further mockery of the fact by ostentatious high living and boasting, and by becoming even more dissolute. The fruits of his life as lover, husband, and gentleman farmer then ripen fully: his wife gives birth to a child fathered by the hired hand; the maid bears his child; and at his doorstep is laid a child that—as is later revealed in *Courasche*—springs from a clandestine union of Simplicius and Courasche's maid. The wife's death concludes the chapter. Simplicius must then act as father to the dishonorable foundling, with his only legitimate child (in Lippstadt) denied him. Likewise, his farmer's role is cast off by turning his property over to his former foster parents.

Grimmelshausen reveals the above rapid sequence of roles to be a unit when, at the beginning of Chapter 11, he sums it up while contemplating the place where he had met his wife:

. . . at just the same place I made the beginning, changed from a free fellow to a slave of love; since then, I have been transformed from an officer into a farmer, from a rich farmer into a poor nobleman, from a Simplicius into a Melchior, from a widower into a husband, from a husband into a cuckold, and from a cuckold again into a widower; thus I had gone from farmer's son to the son of an honorable soldier, and again to a son of my Knan.

All these recapitulated roles have again been shown to be futile. No others are indicated as promising—with one exception, that of a studious recluse, which is developed later.

Conspicuously absent in the above sequence is the practice of medicine. It is, then, probably no accident that this becomes the main subject of discussion in Chapter 11. Simplicius here converses with two patients at the spa. The upshot is a vehement denunciation of physicians, qualified by approval of the use of mineral springs for healing. With this partial rejection of a former role, Simplicius is momentarily in a vacuum, but he immediately resolves to fill it by taking a totally new direction, for which the learned profession of medicine is a stepping-stone:

I resolved to engage in philosophizing, and to strive for a blessed way of life, especially in order to show regret for my unwillingness to atone, and to strive—as did my deceased father—to reach the highest rungs of virtue.

There follows the Mummelsee episode of Chapters 10 through 18. It is to be noted that this lengthy section constitutes the main body of Simplicius' philosophizing phase—between his resolution to devote himself to the *vita contemplativa* as a way to virtue, and his renunciation thereof in Chapter 19. During this fantasy of a visit to the center of the earth, he is largely passive, listening to the prince of the netherworld creatures tell of their quasi-human Utopia in which the subjects of the realm flourish. Finally, however, Simplicius takes some initiative in the discussion, and, as if donning a mask, adopts a buffooning posture, when the king inquires after the life of man on the surface of the earth. Simplicius now briefly displays the same role as at Hanau, but with a far stronger dose of bitter irony than before; for, like the prince in the previous conversation, he also paints a Utopian image of human society, but with the implication that the truth is actually the opposite.

The final step of the Mummelsee section is Simplicius' unsuccessful second attempt to become a kind of physician, as the proprietor of a mineral spring. That this is a part of his philosophizing phase is clear by juxtaposition, and also well within the scope of the universally learned man that he is attempting to become. When the magic gem that is to create the spring drops out of his pocket in the wrong place, it appears to be a simple accident, but one characteristic of Simplicius' ne'er-do-well destiny. Not to be forgotten, however, is the presence of the six hostile and suspicious men, suggesting the character of the creatures with whom he would have had to deal as their "doctor," and in whom he has lost faith, as shown by his conversation with the Mummelsee prince. Upon returning empty-handed from the subterranean Utopia, he seeks further guidance from books.

Much of the whole gamut of seventeenth-century knowledge is summarily suggested at the beginning of Chapter 19. Then, settling on theology as the ultimate source of true knowledge, Simplicius' thoughts take a peculiar turn. He reads of religiously oriented Utopian communities, organized by the Hungarian Anabaptists, and dreams of modelling a colony of his own after them, but within the fold of the Catholic Church. This Utopianism is clearly an outgrowth of the hopes aroused by the Mummelsee experience. His career as a learned man turned Utopian dreamer comes, however, to an abrupt halt with an apparent triviality. He is reminded by the Knan at the end of Chapter 19 that he would "never get such a bunch of fellows together" for such a community. The dream of living in an ideal society thus collapses, and along with it his role of philosopher. He finds himself once more in a vacuum.

The major action of the novel has now come to an end, for Simplicius has completed all phases of life open to him. Futility seems to reign supreme, and this could be the appropriate time for him to become a hermit. Instead he makes one more series of attempts to live in the world as it is, but in areas that do not seem quite real. What follows—the fantastic adventures in Russia and the Orient—is a second recapitulation of roles. This one, however, is, by its very nature, haphazardly composed, and indicates only by suggestion, and in exotic garb, the totality of his previous experience. Simplicius' efforts become desperately pointless and very remote from what would have been commonly considered to be the "real world" of the time. He is cut loose and set afloat in a realm resembling pure fantasy, not unlike flights into various fairy-tale lands, often at the end of stories created by the German Romantics of a century and a half later.

Again he becomes an ambitious military man, and again there is partial success, both in prestige—for he is treated as a duke in

Moscow—and in prowess, when his daring leadership wins a battle for the Czar against the Tartars. His role as a learned man (with a touch of picaresque cleverness) takes on a new variation when he becomes an engineer for the Czar. After his capture by the enemy, the story is then accelerated to a breathless pace that can only allow the sketchiest of indications of his adventures in the Far East, then in the Near East and Mediterranean, taking him finally home again over thousands of miles and many months, elapsing in the space of a few pages. The total effect of this last section is that of a dying man's terminal symptoms. His life, having consisted of vain attempts to find a place in the world, expires.

Upon becoming a hermit, Simplicius no longer plays a role, for roles are acted out in human society only, in order to achieve the specific aims for which they are adopted. Simplicius can now live according to what he considers as truly essential to his being, and this is found on "the tablet of his soul," on which have been inscribed the precepts of Christianity and his father's three principles of knowing oneself, avoiding bad company, and remaining steadfast. The ultimate truth for Simplicius appears now to be that he is incapable of truly being himself, in this Christian sense, in any of the world's roles. The foundation of his life must thus be radically displaced from the world to God, thereby placing the body of the novel, particularly that part of it which consists of his many roles, into an antithetical relationship with its goal.

Here we have reached the end of the role-sequence interpretation, as well as a limitation that becomes apparent at the conclusion of the novel. For primarily *sub specie aeternitatis,* under the static viewpoint of the narrator looking at his life *in retrospect* and *from without,* Simplicius' adventures are made to appear vacuous and meaningless. In the dynamic course of the novel, with all its irrepressible love of life, worldly wisdom, and joyous realism, something other than the end result of the role-sequence is expressed. Here Grimmelshausen shows himself to be a man of the seventeenth century, whose thought, particularly that expressed in literature, is replete with irreconcilable contradictions.

Otherwise the role-sequence is clearly integrated into the overall plan of the novel, particularly with respect to the scheme of the five books. Throughout Book I, Simplicius is a naive and innocent child, and as such he is a kind of "fool" without a place in society. His initial upbringing is shown to be not quite human —what with the lack of real parents. In the forest, he is humanized in a sense, but remains isolated from society. At Hanau, his position, until the end of Book I, is uncertain. In Book II, he then acquires a definite place in military society: as a kind of court fool with Ramsay; as forager and in various other roles with Colonel Corpes; then again as fool, and as orderly, followed by other steps up the military ranks until he becomes the Huntsman at the end of Book II. In this Book he has been, until the very end, a subordinate. In Book III, he is largely in control, even in command at times, over his immediate environment, first as the Huntsman, then as lover and husband. In Book IV, he is placed into roles by which he is humiliated and subordinated, both in love and in war. Book V finds him, once again, no longer completely dominated by the military, aside from a few brief episodes during the recapitulations. As in Book I, he does not clearly belong to any part of society. This makes possible the recovery of the original innocence that had been abandoned in the midsections of the novel.

In spite of such integration into the overall plan, the role-sequence, considered in isolation, threatens to fragment our image of the novel into abrupt and sometimes arbitrarily arranged pieces. The masks and costumes enhance the novel with colorfulness and variation, but they cannot provide the core of unity that their ubiquitous presence may seem to indicate. There are yet deeper strata to be exposed.

V   *"The Children of the Planets"*

The most important discovery in the studies of *Simplicissimus* published in recent years has been the fact that Grimmelshausen made far greater use of astrological symbols and patterns in his novel than had been previously recognized.[12] The validity of this approach is both historically and biographically well-founded, for Grimmelshausen lived during a Golden Age in European astrology,[13] and his knowledge of this subject was unquestionably extensive and profound.[14] Yet until a few years ago, when another renaissance of astrology occurred in the Western world, its predominant role in his thought and art received very little attention.

Superficially, we have at least a few strong hints of the relevance of the ancient art and science in allusions to the planets. The most outstanding of these is to "Jupiter," the name of the character who is centrally placed in Book III, and who, in his mad harangues, conveys so much of the novel's satirical and critical message. Almost as obvious is the role of "Mars" in Book I, who sits supreme at the pinnacle in the tree allegory of Europe at War. Likewise, Venus plays her well-known role in the Paris episodes of Book IV, where there is even a direct reference to her in the heading of Chapter 4, the "Mount of Venus" episode.

These allusions taken by themselves could, of course, simply be construed as references to Greek and Roman mythology, which overlaps so much with astrology that, at times, the two are extremely difficult to separate. When, however, the specifically astrological symbolism associated with these ancient gods is considered in sequence, a definite pattern emerges that is clearly discernible to anyone knowledgeable in the rudiments of astrology. This pattern has been well established by both Weydt and Rehder.[15] It becomes readily apparent that Grimmelshausen composed his novel according to the "Chaldean order" of the seven bodies in the Solar System that are visible to the naked eye—at that time still the only significant ones known to astronomers and astrologers.

The Chaldean order is the sequence of the seven planets (which, in astrology, include the Sun and Moon) arranged according to their maximum apparent velocities in forward motion through the Zodiac, usually beginning with the most rapid and ending with the slowest, as follows: Moon, Mercury, Venus, Sun, Mars, Jupiter, Saturn. This provides the astrologer with a basic symbolic sequence related particularly to phases of development in *time*. The best-known vestige of this system is the order of the days of the week, named after ancient gods, and derived by means of the strange device of the seven-pointed star.[16] Probably its best-known application among present-day astrologers is the ascription of approximate ages to persons indicated by planets in a horoscope, i.e., the Moon symbolizes an infant; Mercury a child; Venus an adolescent; the Sun a young adult; Mars a person in full maturity; Jupiter one of middle age; and Saturn an elderly person.[17] This, of course, brings Shakespeare's "Seven Ages of Man," the most well-known use of this seven-fold division by age in literature, to mind.[18] Shakespeare takes slight liberties with the sequence. The figure corresponding to Mars (the soldier) and that belonging to the Sun (the judge) are reversed. Furthermore, the Sun is not the most appropriate symbol for a judge, this office being more properly suggested by the wise and beneficent Jupiter. The "lean and slippered pantaloon" is likewise questionable as a Jovian figure. Yet enough of the remainder of the structure is present to make its astrological origin apparent.

Grimmelshausen likewise found it necessary to modify the Chaldean order by reversing it—beginning with Saturn, the slowest planet, and ending with the Moon, the swiftest. He also took the same liberty as Shakespeare: he reversed the order of Jupiter and Mars, for reasons that will become apparent. Thus the sequence of the planetary phases of *Simplicissimus* is as follows: Saturn, Mars, Jupiter, Sun, Venus, Mercury, Moon.[19] This reversal, besides fitting the action of the novel, might well signify the topsy-turvy world of the satirical tradition.

The reversal of Mars and Jupiter places Saturn in juxtaposition with Mars—astrologically a grim combination, aptly symbolizing the misery of Book I. Soon after the story opens, soldiers descend precipitately on the Knan's farm, and ruthlessly pillage, torture, rape, and burn. Thus, early in the story, Saturn (ruling peasants) and Mars (ruling soldiers) come together in woeful "conjunction." After Simplicius' escape, he finds refuge in the crude hut of the forest hermit, his father. The opening phase of the novel is thus predominantly "Saturnian," because Saturn traditionally rules peasants and hermits, since toil and solitude are features of this planet's symbolism. Saturn's negative qualities—in this case punitive ones—manifest themselves in extreme form in the attack on the farm, when combined with "martial" aggression. The reason for the Mars-Jupiter reversal thus becomes apparent: it allows the direct confrontation of peasants and soldiers. As Grimmelshausen states in the beginning of Chapter 4 (that of the attack), he believed the war to be God's just punishment of men for their sins—a Saturnian idea, since to this planet is assigned the role of severe moralist and taskmaster. Later, during Simplicius' two-year stay with his hermit-father, Saturn's more positive qualities are manifested. Simplicius' father is, appropriately, a stern father figure, but the life-style of the two is one of healthful discipline, toil, study, and regular observance of religious duties. Even in Grimmelshausen's time, when so much gloom-and-doom astrology was prevalent, Saturn was not always the "Greater Malefic," as he is traditionally called. Saturn as a more positive symbol is exemplified in Albrecht Dürer's engraving of the "Saturnian" St. Jerome (1514), whose severity is softened by his serenity, as with Simplicius' father.

The Mars phase is foreshadowed by the attack on the farm and predominates after Simplicius leaves the forest. It enters in full force into the dream allegory of Chapters 15 through 18, in which Mars is shown to rule Europe at war by his dominant position at the highest pinnacle. The boy is actually drawn into this world of war when he is captured by soldiers from the nearby fortress of Hanau. At first, he serves, and later he leads, becoming more and more "martial." In the midst of this development, however, the next phase (Jupiter) is anticipated, as was Mars during the Saturn section. Jovian symbolism is manifested when Simplicius plays the role of jester for several chapters (Book I, Chs. 7–13), for Jupiter, the planet of wisdom, rules fool figures, even some madmen, as is consistent with the tradition of wise fools and madmen—seen in Shakespeare and Cervantes. Thus, in the midst of the Mars section, the war and the society that feeds on it are chastised and ridiculed by the "higher mind," a term often used in astrology for Jovian wisdom. Mars prevails, however with the high point of this section reached during the bloody battle of Wittstock (Book II, Ch. 27).

"Jupiter" then appears in the flesh near the beginning of Book III and lays out his paradoxically wise but mad plan for the salvation of Europe. This is an "afflicted" Jupiter, as typified by the negative qualities of this planet—excess, extravagance, and babbling of sheer nonsense. Yet some transcendent wisdom cannot be denied him, for he voices a desire for the long overdue peace in Europe and for an end to the insane religious strife of the time. That this madman is primarily an *astrological* Jupiter, and only secondarily a *mythological* one, can be seen in the following passage:

[76]

The Masterpiece: *The Adventurous Simplicissimus*

I intend to send such a great hero that he will need no soldiers, and yet will reform the whole world. In the hour of his birth, I shall bestow on him a handsome body, stronger than Hercules', and adorn him with abundant foresight, wisdom, and understanding. To this, Venus shall add a comely face that will exceed in beauty that of Narcissus, Adonis, and even my Ganymede; she shall ornament his virtues with a special elegance, charm, and grace; and she will make him pleasing to everyone, because she will be looking upon him ever more kindly in his nativity. Mercury, on the other hand, shall accord him an incomparably ingenious mind. And the inconstant Moon shall not be harmful to him, but useful, for she shall engender in him an incredible swiftness. Pallas shall rear him on Mount Parnassus. And *in Hora Martis,* Vulcan shall forge him a sword, with which he will subdue the whole world, and cut down the Godless. . . . (Book III, Ch. 4)

The planetary gods are thus assigned the task of creating an ideal and heroic type of human being, as would be indicated in an ideally configurated horoscope, or birth-chart. Also the technical terms, "nativity" (German: "Nativität," which to the astrologer means "birth-chart," as in English), and "the Mars hour" reveal the astrological origin of the passage. It is further exemplified by the appropriate ascriptions of the various well-known traits to the planetary gods: Jupiter himself endows the hero with the physical prowess of an athlete (a connotation of the Zodiacal sign of Sagittarius, which Jupiter rules), along with great capabilities of the "higher mind"; Mercury with those of the "lower mind"; Venus with a pleasing appearance, etc.

Jovian symbolism gives cohesion to the first half of Book III. The "Martial" phase being past around the transition from Book II into Book III, Simplicius now behaves mainly in a Jovian way. As the "Huntsman of Soest" (Jupiter ruling the hunt), he manifests the benevolence of Jupiter, the "Greater Benefic," in his Robin Hood role of stealing only from the rich and giving often to the poor. This generosity manifests itself most fully when, at the end of Book II, he lavishly compensates a clergyman for the bacon and sausage he and his men had stolen from him. The first half of Book III traces the increase of Simplicius' wealth (a Jovian motif), culminating in the discovery of the treasure in Chapter 12. Here a positive and negative aspect of Jupiter find themselves in conflict. For the character Jupiter (now, appropriately, playing the role of Simplicius' jester) offers the wise counsel that his master distribute his wealth in order to gain favor among his potential enemies. The "higher mind" is acting here as a deterrent to its own lower tendency to pursue wealth.

During the Jupiter phase, Simplicius becomes increasingly the egocentric focus of attention, benignly shining on the little "Solar System" of soldiers surrounding him. Such behavior is most closely associated with the zodiacal sign of Leo, ruled by the Sun. Thus the next phase, that of the Sun, is increasingly anticipated, then abruptly commences with Simplicius' capture by the enemy at the midpoint of Book III. As a prisoner, he is treated royally, like King Leo himself. On his "leonine" honor not to attempt to escape, he is given freedom of movement within the town of Lippstadt, and takes full advantage of it not only to develop himself as an elegant gentleman but also to engage in amorous pursuit of several of the young ladies of the town, seven of whom become pregnant. Thus this section has a Venusian undercurrent. His "Solar" centrality, however, dominates.

Venus then rises high over the story when, in Book IV, he becomes the favorite of the Paris stage with his acting, singing, and lute-playing—all enhanced in the eyes of the aristocratic ladies by his handsome appearance. The next step is the role of male prostitute, carried out at first with great gusto, then with increasing weariness. The Paris episode, with its sultry atmosphere of extreme Venusian sensuousness, contains probably the most consistent and obvious use of planetary symbolism. The combination of sex, the arts, and the social graces pervades these chapters in the most characteristic manner of Venus—at first appealing and gratifying, then oversatiating and corruptive.

In the remainder of the novel, the planetary symbolism is complicated by some new factors. Most important is that the two remaining phases—those of Mercury and the Moon—are not as clearly distinguishable from each other as the earlier ones, since both connote instability and changeability, which best characterize the pace and development in the remainder of the novel. Therefore they are intermingled more than the others, with only a slight predominance of Mercury over the Moon in the remainder of Book IV, and of the Moon over Mercury in Book V.

Furthermore, Mercury and the Moon are "neutral" in that they take on the connotations and colorations of things in juxtaposition with them; therefore a wider range of symbolism can be expressed. Finally, in the rapidly paced sequence of the mercurial and lunar sections, Grimmelshausen includes the recapitulations already described (see p. 69 ff.).

The instability of Simplicius' life following the Paris experiences is manifested mainly in his wanderings. At first, only Mercury is clearly in evidence as the planetary symbol, for Simplicius' first means of sustenance is his role as a vendor of patent medicines. This mercurial occupation (i.e., medicine in general) is anticipated by his work as assistant to Dr. Canard at the beginning of Book IV. Negatively, Mercury rules liars, charlatans, and thieves. Obviously there is a large element of this negativity in Simplicius' preparation and hawking of his wares. His unstable mercurial course then takes him back to an army garrison, where he is a common soldier, but with an uncommon ability to construct clever gadgets (such as rabbit snares)—a decidedly mercurial talent. In the midst of such episodes, however, Simplicius, in his attempt to make the journey home by water, almost drowns (Book IV, Ch. 10). This is a distinctly *lunar* episode, since the Moon's symbolic moistness and rapid movement are associated with journeys by water.

The chapters dealing with Olivier in the midsection of Book IV are mercurial in their connotation of thievery. A further association with this planet is use of the symbolism of the Twins (Gemini), the zodiacal sign ruled by Mercury. The dual nature of this sign suggests—especially in seventeenth-century astrology —the conflict of good and evil, manifesting itself most graphically in the wrestling match between Simplicius and Olivier. This moral struggle is also present in Simplicius' relations with Olivier and Hertzbruder, Simplicius' friend and guardian angel.

After Olivier's death and Simplicius' reunion with Hertzbruder, a series of chapters (the first eleven of Book V) combines mercurial and lunar symbolism in approximately equal proportions. Also injected are some recapitulative episodes that contain no such symbolism. Most of the high points, however, fit the main pattern. The religious pilgrimage at the opening of Book V is lunar in character. Whether the episodes of great fluctuation in Simplicius' fortunes following this section (especially Chapters 3 and 4) are mercurial or lunar is difficult to determine, but they are certainly at least one or both. Following this, in Chapter 5, Simplicius is expressly identified by Jupiter as "Mercury" in the brief reunion between the two.

Simplicius' stay at the "Sauerbrunnen" spa combines the mercurial practice of medicine with "lunar" cures (i.e., with water) —the Moon being "moist" in nature as well as ruler of the cardinal water sign of Cancer. Mercury remains strongly in evidence until Chapter 19 of Book V, while the lunar symbolism gradually increases, primarily in the presence of its element, water. The rapid succession of ups and downs suggests primarily lunar symbolism: this would include the hero's second marriage, his fathering of three children simultaneously, the loss of his wife, prosperity followed by bankruptcy, going from one study to another, and world travels—all in relatively few pages. The peak of lunar symbolism is reached in the Mummelsee episode, almost all of which takes place in a submarine kingdom. The long journey by water and the imaginary nature of the adventure is clearly under the Moon's rulership. (The Moon rules dreams, the imagination, fantasy, etc.) This is underscored by the express statement that it is the time of the full Moon (Ch. 16). Then follows one brief mercurial chapter when Simplicius retires to a life of study, directed principally toward learning how to establish a Christian Utopia. This all turns out to be "lunar" fantasy when the Knan, with consummate common sense, points out that it is unfeasible because no one will join it.

From this point on, Simplicius has his most unstable and fluctuating series of experiences in the novel as a far-travelling adventurer and soldier of fortune. Here the Moon dominates completely and at her greatest velocity. Upon the return from his travels, and the resumption of his life in the forest, the cycle is completed, and the novel ends under the domination of the stern image of the Saturnian hermit.

The reasons why Grimmelshausen chose to unfold his tale with the aid of the Chaldean sequence can be derived only from indirect evidence, since clear-cut statements about it by him are not extant. First we note that the Chaldean order, which primarily concerns the planets and their motions, comprises that structuring of astrological symbolism which is most dynamic, and is capable of the greatest variation and combination.

The Masterpiece: *The Adventurous Simplicissimus*

Astrology being, in its highest forms, a symbolic cosmology, the Chaldean order is eminently suitable as a way of providing meaningful and all-embracing sequences in an attempt to include a stupendous breadth of experience within the horizons of seventeenth-century Germany.

The ultimate aim of the novel is to take the hero through a series of experiences that convince him that "all is vanity." One of the most effective narrative techniques employed for that aim is the constant increase in *pacing*, so that Simplicius' life at the end is a frenetic, headlong dash after ever more transitory goals —vanity in its extreme. Astrology makes the greatest contribution to this pacing, for the sequence of the planets from Saturn through the Moon lends a peculiarly appropriate and meaningful order to the tale and, along with it, most of the beauty of its ever-increasing rhythms.

There are points at which Grimmelshausen departs from, or even expresses opposition to, astrology, and these are important to note for a full and unbiased picture of the novel. We may wonder whether he was expressing his own wavering attitude toward that subject when in Book V, Ch. 19 he has Simplicius impatiently renounce it, because he has found it—along with other studies—"false and uncertain." This might well be interpreted in the context of Simplicius', not Grimmelshausen's, mercurial and lunar instability. Yet it is to be noted that Grimmelshausen himself entertained at least occasional doubts, as shown by such statements in *The Perpetual Calendar* as: "it [nativity reading] is as uncertain and unstable as Mercury and the Moon themselves".[20] This refers, it must be added, only to one *part* (though the most well-known one) of the art. Thus it is not really inconsistent with the veritable hymn to astrology which is sounded in another passage:

. . . it is founded upon the mysteries of nature and is ordained by God the Almighty for His praise, without human fictions. . . . It is a special gift . . . a ladder whereby our understanding climbs into the heavenly firmament.[21]

We may conclude that Grimmelshausen's attitudes toward astrology ranged from wholehearted approval to mild disapproval. And there are important matters *not* closely relevant to the planetary symbolism, such as the satirical and ironical dimensions, to be discussed in the next section. The most clearly positive ac-complishment of the astrological structure is that it enriches the work with the magnificent cosmology that astrology offered to the Renaissance and Baroque ages, and which it can offer to us with the aid of some preknowledge and deciphering. As exalted a purpose as this structure may have, it is incorrect to equate the valid symbolic representation of a cosmology with the writing of a great work of fiction. With modifications and very special utilization of planetary symbolism, Grimmelshausen made even this huge and intricate system subservient to the artistic totality of the novel.

VI *"Telling the Truth with a Laugh"*

Despite grim Saturn's embrace of the first five books of *Sim-plicissimus*, Grimmelshausen emphatically asserts that, in his novel, he is "telling the truth with a laugh" (see p. 41). In this connection, certain major passages remain to be discussed in greater detail and from a different point of view. These are predominantly satirical, and include the opening description of peasant life (Book I, Ch. 1–2); the "Tree of Society" (Book I, Ch. 15–18); Simplicius' social criticism while a jester at Hanau (Book I, Ch. 19 through Book II, Ch. 14); the main Jupiter episode (Book III, Ch. 3–6); and the "Mummelsee" chapters (Book V, Ch. 12–17). The most emphatic and closely interrelated passages are those symmetrically arranged in Books I, III, and V, for they are clearly allegorical visions having wide-ranging rele-vance.[22]

It is readily apparent that in *Simplicissimus* there are two main kinds of satire: that which ridicules particular conditions and customs in seventeenth-century Germany; and the universal kind that reveals man as the great fool of Creation, and his world as being topsy-turvy. Upon initial consideration of these catego-ries, it should be apparent that, toward the beginning, the first kind prevails, and toward the end, the second.

The very first sentence of Book I emphasizes contemporary conditions: "There is appearing *in this age of ours* (of which people believe that it is the last) a disease among common people . . ." (italics mine). The narrator then proceeds to de-scribe certain people afflicted by this "disease," who dress and behave in an aristocratic manner that is incongruous with their humble origins. The satirical theme and tone of the opening segment—the first three chapters—are thus established. Simplicius' role and environment in the peasantry are first described in terms that connote a comic portrayal of country bumpkins. At least he would be taken as such a figure by the higher classes. This type of satire is a common feature of Spanish picaresque novels, with which the opening passage has been linked (though indirectly; see p. 42 f.). In Chapter 3, however, the vantage point is shifted to one of great sympathy with the peasants' lot of poverty and servitude.

This dichotomy of attitude remains unresolved throughout the novel, unless one considers the final renunciation of the whole world, with its inevitable social injustice, as a resolution. What follows in Chapter 4 is a grisly demonstration of the truth of Simplicius' song in Chapter 3. Soon all that is left of the satire are a few instances of "gallows humor" stemming from Simplicius' naive lack of awareness of the full extent of the suffering around him.

The amoral naiveté is partially dispelled in the next several chapters by Simplicius' Christian education.[23] Thereafter of course, the habitual observance of the rituals of the faith is extremely difficult in the demoralizing chaos of the Thirty Years' War, as is implicit in the dream of the "Tree of Society" following Simplicius' serene isolation from that society. In its use of the dream for visions of mankind, grotesquely transformed for satirical purposes, this episode is a well-known device, as in Moscherosch's *Philander von Sittewald.* Such satire is by no means designed to evoke good-natured laughter, but at best a wry smile in recognition of bitter truths.

A single idea stands out here: the cruel injustice perpetrated on the lowly who, in the dream, bear the whole weight of the tree at the bottom, while the military occupies the tree, with relative height determining rank. This commiseration with the peasants and common soldiers makes up the strand of the satire of Chapter 3. One of its salient features is the slippery trunk between commissioned officers and the lower ranks. Of the latter, very few manage to bridge this gap between the nobles and the commoners, which is even greater in the military than in civilian life. The debate that ensues between an officer of the nobility and a commoner sergeant comprises the main body of the vision. Up to the end of the discussion, it appears as if the sergeant might win at least a moral victory with superior arguments. The outcome, however, is inconclusive, for Simplicius says of the sergeant at the end: "I didn't care to listen to the old jackass any more, but rather granted him willingly the cause of his complaints, since he often lashed the poor soldiers like dogs." Thus the conflict remains unresolved, with moral right and wrong divided between the officer and sergeant. The ambiguity of Simplicius' later elevation is thus prepared for. As in the first three chapters, the satire is ambiguously directed at representatives of both sides in this sharply divided society.

The great destructiveness of the war is shown when the individual trees clash in battle, causing men to be knocked off the branches in droves. Thus all of Europe is likewise divided. But in another sense, Europe is also *united* in this nightmare, as is shown when the forest is transformed into one gigantic tree, with Mars perched at the top. Indeed, it appears as if it could cast a shadow beyond Europe over the whole world. The dream, then, succinctly pictorializes the historical situation of the seventeenth-century world. It is reality concentrated and elevated into surreality. Its nightmarish qualities would make it unlikely that Simplicius would immediately join forces with it. This is important to consider in the next satirical episodes in which Simplicius is a jester. Here he is *in* the world of this dream, but not yet *of* it. The two roles of fool—the one before, the other after his transformation by Ramsay—govern two different kinds of satire. The first is directed at *sin,* and the second at *folly*.

The first stage is depicted in Book I, Chapters 24 through 27, Simplicius introduces this segment with the statement that "at that time, nothing more estimable could be found in me than a clean conscience, and a genuinely pious disposition." Repugnance at the behavior of those surrounding him is his prevailing attitude. The moral basis is exclusively Christian, manifested in explicit condemnations of those who do the faith mere lip service and habitually violate it. There follows a lengthy catalogue of sins. The image of Christ punctuates the ending of the chapter, leading into Chapter 25, which concentrates on Christian love, or rather its absence. The first half deals with lack of neighborly love, especially as evidenced by violent outbursts of hate; the second half with profanity—violations of the commandment to love God. Finally, in Chapter 27, after briefly satirizing the Secretary's lucrative and otherwise profitable art of writing, Simplicius turns to a condemnation of a book of titles, used as a reference book for such things as formal epistolary salutations. These pompously Baroque titles provide an obvious target for satirical ridicule from Simplicius' Christian point of view, the satire being directed at the underlying sinful pride of such practices. As he says to the Secretary, the noblemen addressed with such exalted titles, after all, "are all children of Adam, of one common origin —that is, of dust and ashes. 'Most Sacred,' 'Most Invincible,' 'Most Illumined,'—are these not divine characteristics?" It is precisely this sin of which Simplicius is most guilty later on as the Huntsman of Soest. At this point, however, he is still an innocent child who appears not only naive to his surroundings, but downright offensive. This is aptly symbolized by the stench that he inadvertently wafts into the Secretary's nose—an impressive finale of the first phase of Simplicius' fool's satire.

The second phase consists of Chapters 9 through 13 of Book II. As a result of the attempts to drive him made, he has cause to alter his fool's role greatly. This somewhat more "mercurial" phase is dominated by wit and cleverness. Herewith the angle of attack is shifted from Christian to rational principles. The beginning is Simplicius' debut as "mad" fool in polite society, with elegant ladies of the nobility present. He bursts brilliantly into the scene with the pyrotechnics of his "cockeyed praise of a noble lady." Her artificiality, her excesses in costume and adornment, and her immodesty (bared breasts, according to the *a la mode* custom of the time) are mercilessly pointed up and "praised" with terms and metaphors derived from the peasantry. (This incongruity of language and subject matter, incidentally, is the reverse of that in Book I, Chapters 1–3.) The satire is merciless; yet it evokes peals of laughter from his audience, and Simplicius reaches a certain height of glory here. He then finds himself in a defensive position in Chapter 10, when he and the Secretary resume their debate about titles of nobility. This chapter is overladen with learned examples of great men whose deeds deserved such rewards as dignifying titles. Simplicius' argumentation takes a new turn when he condemns achievement in war, for its cost in blood, along with a wide range of other achievements (such as in arts and crafts), because they are "nothing but vanity and folly."

In the next chapter (11), Simplicius pursues a similar line in his characterization of Ramsay's position as being hopelessly overburdened with care and guilt, and of his own "calf's" role as free and happy. Again the *vanitas* theme is sounded. The realm of Simplicius' bliss is then extended to the animal kingdom, in which life moves by instinct and in harmony among all creatures and with nature. This arouses suspicion in his listeners that he might be sane, or—much worse—is practicing black magic. The latter motif casts a new light on his worldly wisdom. By now, much of his former innocence is gone, and motifs associated with the devil (such as black magic) forewarn of Simplicius' later entanglements with evil. This dark cloud at the beginning of Chapter 13 is soon dispelled, however, when Simplicius moves his audience to tears with his fervent prayer. Thus the satire culminates in a return to Christian piety, by means of which the rationally viewed secular matters just discussed are transcended. The *vanitas* theme has been expounded in the light of both faith and reason.

The effect of a return to God in a godless world is momentary, and attention is soon directed toward Simplicius' future at Hanau—for which, ironically, worldly happiness is promised. When he is captured by the Croatians in Chapter 14, it is the beginning of his full integration into the world of the Thirty Years' War. From this point on, considerable irony is present, for from now on Simplicius does precisely what he has been condemning. This becomes especially apparent at the next peak of satire in Book III. By the time of Jupiter's dazzling performance, Simplicius has been corrupted by the world, and Jupiter's moralizings are a strangely logical continuation of those of the former "fool." An intrinsic relationship between the two men is made explicit when Simplicius remarks, after Jupiter has joined him in Book III, Chapter 8: "Thus I came to have my own fool—without even having to buy one—though I myself had been obliged to be one just a year before."[24] There is, of course, an important difference between the two: now the hopes for a better world are voiced not by a fool feigning to be mad, but by a patently deranged crackpot, whose expansive idealizings are constantly being deflated by the suppressed giggles of his audience, by his incongruous obscenities and above all, by his sudden descent from glory in Chapter 6, when he pulls his trousers down in order to get at his fleas. It may be tempting to oversimplify on the basis of his ridiculous qualities, and deny him all true significance. This would be wrong, however, for he is later presented in a very sympathetic light, as when he wisely counsels Simplicius to give away his wealth in order to win friends (Book III, Ch. 13). Also, as with Don Quixote, there are times when the reader cannot help but desire the attainment of the good-natured madman's ideals, and to grant him the madman's peculiar kind of wisdom amidst his ravings.

In fact, Jupiter's ideas are singularly penetrating. He offers, above all, profound commentary on his times, especially in Chapter 4 and 5, which neatly divide the matter into the secular and the religious. The need for peace being paramount, Jupiter first outlines his plans to create a Great German Hero who will bring about and enforce peace, then unify all of Europe under a German Emperor. The Germanic nations would (of course!) agree to it out of a sense of ethnic brotherhood, the other peoples of Europe following suit, since in the past they had all been ruled by Germanic lords anyway. As absurd as this plan may seem, there is a great deal of good sense (or at least historical sense) attendant upon this madness. In the first place, Europeans on both sides in the conflict had reason to place hopes on many a "Great German Hero"—a series of powerful political and military leaders, including two Holy Roman Emperors (Ferdinand II and III), King Gustavus Adolphus of Sweden, Wallenstein, Mansfeld, and Bernhard von Weimar. And the empire Jupiter has in mind is not far removed from the once powerful and multinational Holy Roman Empire. Once and for all someone—anyone—would have been welcomed to win a decisive victory, so that the gruesome stalemate that was to last for three decades could be ended.

Likewise, according to Jupiter, the religious conflict that is one of the causes of the war would be settled simply by mutual consent of all parties. Those who refuse, as he interjects in his grimly humorous naiveté, shall be summarily martyred. The serious idea underlying this notion would be the assumption of a supradenominational Christianity, which Grimmelshausen at times espoused, and which is aptly commented on by Logau in his often-cited satirical epigram: "Lutheran, Papist, Calvinistic —these three faiths are with us; but there is doubt as to where Christianity is."[25] Jupiter's manner of handling the religious problem is, of course, further removed from historical reality than are his ideas relating to the secular realm, for nothing in the seventeenth century seems so futile as an ecumenical movement, and some chief proponents thereof appear to be all but insane.[26]

Jupiter's megalomaniacal pomposity gives rise to Simplicius' verbal attack on him, in which he taunts him, saying that this king of Olympus and the whole company of Greek gods were, after all, a pack of libertines, scoundrels, and villains. The result of this invective is the delightful burlesque of Chapter 6, in which Jupiter's fevered imagination creates the fantasy of the fleas who have entered into negotiations with him for improved treatment by the ladies. Thus in the transition from Chapter 5 to 6 we have not only a precipitous descent, but also a sudden diminution of the scope of Jupiter's vision, shrinking a grandiose macrocosm into one of the smallest of visible "worlds"—that of the fleas. Surely, this is one of the most destructive trivializations of which satire is capable. In spite of the profound seriousness underlying Jupiter's Utopian vision, in the end the whole dream is easily dispelled by a deflating realism.

There has been some disagreement concerning the literary and historical sources of Jupiter, as tantalizing and evocative as he is. He naturally evokes associations with *Don Quixote*, the Utopian tradition, and many figures of the madman throughout literature. As yet, however, scholars have been unable to prove beyond doubt the existence of a specific source for this magnificent figure, although a number of intriguing possibilities have been advanced.[27]

In the context of the whole novel, Jupiter can be viewed from three main perspectives. First and foremost, he is, in the main body of his harangue, pointing out the absurdity of the strife-torn world of his time. Secondly, Simplicius, now entangled in this world, is also implicitly satirized. (As has been indicated, the Simplicius of Book III is failing to practice what he himself had preached when cast in the role of a "fool.") Thirdly, Jupiter unconsciously satirizes himself, with his obvious megalomania, the "battle of the fleas," and his incongruous obscenities. Thus the total satire of the Jupiter episode adds up to a highly ambivalent set of statements: the world is ridiculed for being engaged in the folly of war; Jupiter, however, is himself engaging in folly in his attempts to correct that of the world. All is vanity, even the efforts to resist vanity. Consistent with this idea is Simplicius' failure to recognize Jupiter's more positive wisdom for many chapters thereafter. In fact, not until the middle of Book V, the final section of the satirical portion, does wisdom assert itself so strongly again.

The context of this "Mummelsee" adventure in Book V is especially important, for the episode is the first step in realizing Simplicius' resolution to devote himself to philosophy and lead a "blessed way of life." The journey to the center of the earth is immediately followed by his pursuit of more conventional studies, ending with theology, with a peculiar emphasis on Utopian religious communities. Again, in a new way, he is given a macrocosmic view of the world, as in the "Tree of Society" dream and in Jupiter's visions.

The frame of reference of his philosophizing is largely constituted by the Paracelsian doctrine of the "elemental spirits" of fire, earth, air, and water (salamanders, pygmies, sylphs, and nymphs, respectively).[28] Although Grimmelshausen modified the traditional system somewhat (his underwater creatures are sylphs instead of nymphs), its basic meaning remains the same: it is part of a symbolic cosmology, this time embracing nature and the earth as a whole, rather than having prime reference to seventeenth-century man, as in the other two main satirical sections. It should be noted here that the four "elements" not only comprise an all-embracing scientific system, but they were also totally and harmoniously integrated with another and far more extensive cosmology of the time—the astrological system.[29]

Simplicius' "plunge" into philosophy via the Mummelsee provides a grand metaphor suggestive of something akin to a Faustian urge to discover what "holds the world together at its innermost core." Somewhat as Goethe does in Part II of *Faust*, Grimmelshausen engages here in playful fantasy in his quest. Colorful creatures entertain us, but, at the end, provide us with the most profound of insights. Simplicius' manner of summoning the sylphs by throwing rocks into the water, the magic emerald that enables him to breathe beneath its surface, and all the other pansophistic and alchemistic mumbo-jumbo serve, however, not only to delight, but also to indicate the esoteric nature of the mysteries into which Simplicius is being initiated. That this is indeed "another world"—with an altogether different, nonhuman population—is then clearly revealed and underscored when the basic nature of the "sylphs" is explained to Simplicius in Chapter 13.

The differences between them and the people of the surface center around their lack of a soul. Out of this fact emerges a set of the sharpest possible contrasts. Sylphs do not suffer either agony or ecstasy; man's lot is little else but that, with more emphasis on the agony. Sylphs therefore die painlessly but with total extinction, like a candle flame being extinguished; men suffer death pangs but live on in a hereafter. Sylphs are free; while men are literally or figuratively enslaved. In the last analysis, however, man is "ennobled and blessed to a far higher degree by our Creator" than the sylphs, for a blissful eternity and the privilege of seeing God face-to-face forever are ultimately, when deserved, bestowed on him.

The pendulum then swings back, in Chapter 14, from seriousness to mildly entertaining erudition, mixed with fantasy concerning things geological and alchemistic. Then, in the crucial Chapter 15, the true satirical aim of the whole episode becomes apparent: the dramatic confrontation with man as he actually is, and also envisaged from the vantage point of a Utopia. In the dialogue of this chapter, the king of the sylphs, who is concerned about God's possible destruction of the world because of man's wrongdoings, asks Simplicius how well persons of various stations in society are fulfilling their missions. Simplicius, suddenly adopting the role of the satirical buffoon, answers with an ingenious kind of *double entendre* that is eminently worthy of the clever fool of Book II. On the surface, he tells a most outrageous pack of lies in describing each representative of his station in society as acting perfectly according to God's will, and consistent with all reasonable demands. Human society, in other words, is ironically whitewashed as a Utopia. In the terms of the novel, Simplicius is deliberately falsifying a world that is more aptly represented by the "Tree of Society," and he is implicitly mocking the naive assumptions, such as Jupiter's, that would seem to make reform feasible. As far as the king is concerned, Simplicius is telling a merciful lie. For the reader, the passage painfully points up the truly corrupt nature of society as Simplicius views it. Thus we have here a peculiar variation on the main theme of Grimmelshausen's later satirical piece, *The Topsy-Turvy World (Die verkehrte Welt)*.

Yet is there perhaps a remote chance that it could all be otherwise? Simplicius must be asking this question implicitly. We know from his past that he is nearly incapable of learning a lesson from experience. This is demonstrated again when he asks the sylphs for a spa on his property, thus transplanting at least a small piece of Utopia into his own life that could possibly benefit others. The magic stone he receives for the purpose at first seems to bear promise of fulfillment of his relatively modest hope. But no sooner has he returned to the surface, when he encounters some particularly un-Utopian human beings—the Swabian farmers who fit the pattern of human society suggested by the ironical description given to the sylph king. Irony is compounded by irony when the magic stone then falls to the ground and creates the spring at a useless location. Even this, however, does not end Simplicius' Utopian aspirations, for he then daydreams about founding a community after the model of the Hungarian Anabaptists; but, like Jupiter's impractical dreams of a better future, the plan is wafted away easily, this time by the Knan's simple remark that probably no one would be interested in joining such a group. The tree of society, as depicted in Book I, still remains standing, even though all religious and rational considerations reveal its evil nature. This is the emphatically whimpering end of the sequence of the three satirical allegories, accompanied by a sardonic smile of recognition of the bitter truth that is left behind. The humorous sweet covering of this didactic pill turns out, in the end, to be quite thin.

When the reader surveys the whole novel in retrospect, he is thoroughly prepared for the viewpoint of the hermit-narrator who has rejected his former self and activities. Here his life can no longer be a laughing matter, as it often has been in the past. Now we can perceive that all along the author has been —paradoxically—undermining his satire, to the extent that he creates a kind of "satire of satire." This is especially true in view of the bathos in Jupiter's descent from his sublime visions to the battle of the fleas. When Grimmelshausen is not satirizing his own satire, he is somehow roundly rejecting what could be, but is not, its ultimate aim: the ridicule of sin and folly for the purpose of founding an ideally blameless and reasonable human society. The vanity of such thinking is fully exposed with the flash-in-the-pan preoccupation with the Hungarian Anabaptists, and its context.

It is essential, in other words, to be aware of the essential irony[30] (including self-irony) underlying the satirical allegories and expressed most pointedly through Simplicius' ill-fated Utopian yearnings. The hero's severely ironical portrayal of mankind to the king of the sylphs is then by no means the only example of satirical *double entendre*: in fact, one can draw a broad analogy between this mode of expression in the episode and that of the other satirical allegories. Since these are, as shown, emphatic anchor points of the novel, they cast their satirical light on the whole work. Face value and real value are often quite different from—or even opposites—to one another. To be noted in this connection is that the words *Der Wahn betreügt* ("Delusion deceives") appear repeatedly as a motto on Grimmelshausen's illustrations to his novel. The supreme example of this is Simplicius' condition in Book III, which appears to be the zenith, but is actually the nadir of his career.[31] Thus, with the possible exception of Christian self-denial, not one fundamental proposal, advanced as a possible solution for a better life, escapes being ironically rejected: wealth, honor, fame, love, marriage, friendship, learning, and industry—all fail to provide more than temporary satisfaction. The more magnificent they appear in their temporal glory, the greater is their indictment from the supratemporal point of view, underscored by the final, severe rejection of the world by the hermit.

A satirical novel? Yes, indeed, but with a strangely contradictory twist. Satire climaxes at certain—though not all—emphatic points in the novel, whereas the sections between them have widely varying degrees of correlation with them. But, above all, the term "satirical novel" must be qualified with the recognition that this satire, powerful as it is, is superseded by the repudiation not only of its target, but also of its weapon.

VII   *Ecclesiastes and the Tragelaph*

Having been analyzed in so many different ways, *Simplicissimus* may appear, at this point, to be an odd composite of divers beasts, like the creature that Grimmelshausen first places before our eyes when we open the novel to the frontispiece. In view of the seeming disparity among the parts, it may be tempting to rest the case with Newald's statement that "the history of literary forms stands helpless before such a Tragelaph."[32] This would mean that it is futile to attempt a correlation of the total form of this novel (however that might be summed up) with a coherent tradition and set of contemporary trends. The implication seems to be that the work has no genuine organic unity. Newald then proceeds, however, to analyze the *individual* plan of the novel (without reference to its place in literary history) as it is revealed in the sequences and interrelationships of its five books. The matter of form remains controversial, however, as can be ascertained immediately upon comparing this description with Scholte's, Alt's, and Weydt's discussions—to mention only a few outstanding examples.[33] These critics' divergent views may be considered as representative of all other formal analyses of *Simplicissimus*.

Since the questions of form and structure are so problematical, it seems best, in attempting to determine its coherence, to proceed from its theme, even though this, too, is somewhat difficult to summarize. To begin with, we have at least the astute observation of Günther Weydt that "all interpreters" of *Simplicissimus* . . . agree at least on one point: that this novel is about the *instability of the world*" ("Unbeständigkeit der Welt").[34] This is partially corroborated by two main points made in this chapter: that the end result of Simplicius' attempts to find his place in "the world" (before fleeing to the forest) is a highly unstable shifting from one role to another; and that the protean nature of this life is underscored by the two astrological symbols dominating most of the last two books—Mercury and the Moon, both signifying inconstancy. The counterforce is the stability of the saturnine hermit.

The end of a novel, however, is not necessarily the bearer of its total theme. Another section, Book III, is at least equally emphatic, but it is not characterized so much by instability. Here Simplicius finds himself in relatively secure, if not unchanging, circumstances. There are, to be sure, warnings that his power and his glory will not last, but they are primarily anticipatory. What does characterize him at this stage is his folly and sinfulness. Also, Jupiter's presence as the "Greater Fortune" suggests the association with "Fortuna," the more "fortuitous" happenings that this goddess brings about, such as the discovery of the hidden treasure. Fortuna was then, as always to some extent, regarded as a fickle trollop, making of her admirers' lives a senseless series of rises and falls. All these things—instability, sin, folly, and Fortuna's ups and downs—are readily subsumed by the many-sided theme of *vanity*, the emptiness revealed at the core of life when viewed in the detached manner of the hermit, *sub specie aeternitatis*. This theme is ubiquitous in the literature of the century, finding its most succinct and intense expression in the lyrics of Gryphius and Hoffmanswaldau, but nowhere as exhaustively as in *Simplicissimus*.

Returning to the formal aspects of the novel, the question is whether the vanity theme sets the overall pattern. It should be noted that this theme presupposes two points of view—the mundane and the supramundane. From the first, life takes on the appearance of an irresistibly beautiful temptress; from the second, a hollow shell. As the story is described on the title page, it is about a human being who begins his life being not yet in the world, then enters it, lives in it temporarily, and then leaves it. The novel is thus embraced at the beginning and the end by the detached point of view described above; between them there is experience in the thick of things without this perspective (except when occasionally injected by the narrator).

The pattern, simply stated, is the "rise" of a man's life—one gigantic wave of fortune, reaching a height of vitality, but also of vanity—and then a fall, whereby he returns at the end, to the original state of rest and innocence. This description, based on that of the title page, is amplified by the verse on the frontispiece, where the hero describes his travels as being all-encompassing (i.e., through all four "elements"), and his book as teaching the reader to "desist from folly and live in peace," as he himself has done. Again, the vanity theme—focussing, this time, on the world's "folly"—is fundamental.

As an enlightening comparison, Gryphius' play *Leo Armenius* offers a contemporary parallel. This play can be similarly diagrammed as a "wave of fortune" in Leo's political career, with another one to come after the end of the play in the life of his adversary, Michael Balbus. Thus the *vanitas* theme is predictably all-pervasive. It would be amiss here, however, not to differentiate between the sombre Gryphius and the satirical and vital Grimmelshausen. The joy and light that often shine through some of the most "vain" sections of *Simplicissimus* were, for Gryphius, rare experiences indeed. Under the surface, an invincible, throbbing drive and an insatiable hunger for life are richly in evidence in this earth-bound Grimmelshausen. It is almost a truism to say that, intermittently, a denial of life, regarding it as "vanity," can make it all the brighter and sweeter upon returning to it. This is the effect of the dark, contrasting mood of the saturnine hermit haunting the background.

What is most shattering for the severely moralistic judgments on the part of the hermit is that, soon after retiring to the forest for a supposedly permanent state of tranquility, we find Simplicius, at the beginning of the first sequel (or "Book VI"), up to his old tricks again, in new guises. Furthermore, there is, later on, the appealing variation on "living in peace"—quite different from the hermit's life—in *Springinsfeld* where Simplicius leads the good life as an upright and respected burgher, yet serene, among his fellow citizens.

The interpretation of the novel on the basis of the *vanitas* theme and its wavelike form does not, we must admit, join seamlessly all the heterogeneous pieces of which it consists. This may well be an impossible task for the critic, in view of the greatly divergent paths taken in previous criticism: and it may not be especially purposeful, anyway. This multifaceted, multistructured work still—in spite of its "disunities"—manages to embrace, within a few hundred pages, an enormous mass of human experience, with appropriately grandiose artistic means, and with at least an overall sense of the elusive wholeness of life. In this novel, with all its vastly suggestive power, life teems and moves in all directions. When a novelist achieves that goal, the chase after the hobgoblin of formal and thematic consistency is small-minded indeed.

CHAPTER 4

The Sequels to Simplicissimus

I *Continuations, Complements, or Supplements?*

THE five-book novel of *Simplicissimus* is "complete" in many ways, as should be apparent from the previous chapter. Yet Grimmelshausen chose not to let his hero and his tale remain in the sombre state of affairs encountered at the end of Book V. In fact, he immediately proceeded to write his first Simplician sequel within a few months of the first edition of the main novel,[1] and continued to produce sequels intermittently almost until the very end of his life, seven years later. The net result is a series of five additional "books," each somewhat longer than the average Book in the original novel. Thus the "trunk novel"[2] is expanded to more than twice its original length, with the sequels constituting Books VI through X of the total Simplician cycle. All the sequels were published singly in Grimmelshausen's lifetime, with the exception of the *Continuation* (or Book VI), which could be obtained either separately or bound together with the second edition of *Simplicissimus*.

In the foreword to the fifth and final sequel, Grimmelshausen explicitly states that the work to follow is the "tenth part or book of *The Life of the Adventurous Simplicissimus*—assuming, that is, that *Courage* is regarded as the seventh book, *Springinsfeld* as the eighth, and the first part of *The Miraculous Bird's Nest* as the ninth. . . ." It is implicit, then, that the book entitled *Continuation* constitutes the sixth part. To be considered also —though not mentioned by Grimmelshausen—are the four brief pieces entitled *First, Second,* and *Third Continuation,* and the *Supplement* which follow Book VI in the fifth edition of *Simplicissimus*. This whole body of writings, then, as the author goes on to say, "is interdependent," and "neither the whole *Simplicissimus* nor one of the latter above-mentioned writings can be adequately understood without thus combining them."[3]

As unequivocal as this statement appears to be on the surface, certain circumstances speak against accepting all its possible implications. After all, Grimmelshausen was viewing his ten-book opus *in retrospect*. His original plan may well have *not* included the sequels. Thus scholarly opinion on the interrelationships of the books ranges from Streller's conviction that I through X form a tightly integrated unit to Scholte's view that the sequels were motivated by purely economic considerations—exploiting the great popularity of *Simplicissimus*—and that, structurally, they are to be viewed as separate units of varying literary merit and representing different genres.[4]

It would be helpful if we could establish, from evidence supplied by the trunk novel, at what point or points Grimmelshausen clearly anticipated the sequels. Unfortunately there is no such evidence. The most meaningful indication in *Simplicissimus* is in the next to last sentence of Book V: "Whether I, however, will endure it [i.e., the hermit's life] until my death, as my deceased father did, is uncertain." Thus the way for Simplicius' return to society is left open. But, as he himself says, the matter is *uncertain*. Furthermore, judging by this statement alone, the idea of writing sequels could have occurred to him as he was approaching the end of his novel, thus leaving it largely intact as an independent work. If we move further back to the chapters containing the minor characters who become the major figures of Books VII and VIII (Courage and Springinsfeld, respectively), we find food for conjecture only. In Books II and III Springinsfeld is portrayed as fully as is necessary in his role of picaresque companion to the Huntsman of Soest, but no more. The full extent of Springinsfeld's meanness and villainy, as exposed in VIII, is hardly apparent. As for Courage, her name and true background are conspicuously absent in the trunk story. Yet her participation in the incidents concerning Simplicius' three almost simultaneously born children, may have been designed for later amplification. But this is hardly provable; nor is any other assumption as to the time of conception of Books VI through X. The question of interdependence must be answered largely from the sequels themselves.

II   *The* Continuation *of 1668*

The *Continuation* or Book VI, was not only Grimmelshausen's
first work after the completion of *Simplicissimus*, but also his
first literary product as mayor of Renchen. There has been much
speculation as to the motivation for the great speed (a few
months at most) with which he wrote it.[5] The strongest possibility so far suggested is that it was expedited in order to lend
additional appeal to the second edition of the novel after the
immediate success of the first, particularly in response to the
literary pirates. Another important factor was the publication
of a work that was to become the major source of the *Continuation*—namely Henry Nevil's *The Isle of Pines*, an early
"Robinson Crusoe" type of story first appearing in English, then
rapidly spreading throughout Europe in translation in 1668. The
question of source or influence is slightly complicated by the
fact that Grimmelshausen also derived some details from a travel-
book, published in 1600, which in all likelihood he had read
before *The Isle of Pines* became available.[6] The haste with which
the *Continuation* was written is reflected in the fact that it
contains a greater amount of verbatim quotations from these and
other books than any of the other Simplician writings.[7]

The first impression made by the *Continuation* as a whole is
likely to be—to say the least—one of heterogeneity. The tale begins with Simplicius dwelling in his sylvan hermitage of Book V.
At first, his moral severity, reflected in the rationalizations of
his humor as mere sweetening of the bitter didactic pill, is typical
of his Saturnian phase. This soon dissolves, however, in the appearance of a new aspect of his character, that of sloth. His long
allegorical dream showing Greed, Extravagance, and related
figures in Hell, plotting against mankind, removes us for many
pages from Simplicius' immediate concerns—more so than the
allegories of the trunk novel. Even more remote is the story of
Julus and Avarus, who are possessed by the hellish spirits of
Extravagance and Greed. Somehow this leads us into Simplicius'
encounter in the woods with the allegorical "Baldanders" ("Ever-
changing"), whom the hermit promptly emulates in his decision
to become a pious mendicant. A series of adventurous travels
ensues, with no particular principle of sequence immediately in
evidence, except to cause Simplicius to sin again (by possessing
money and telling tall tales), and to get him shipwrecked and

marooned on a desert isle. He is a new kind of hermit and his piety is fully developed, partly by contrast with his companion, the carpenter (who eventually dies), partly as a result of his new environment. Then, for the first time, it is revealed that *Simplicissimus* and the *Continuation* have been written on palm leaves and shipped back to Europe via a Dutch sea-captain!

Whimsical as this potpourri may be, a few ways as to how it supplements the trunk novel are immediately apparent. Here mankind is in a state of peace throughout. Yet Simplicius chooses to remain a hermit at the end—the implication being that the *vanitas* of living in human society holds true in peace as well as in war. The relationship with the novel is even more specific, for on closer examination we find that the *Continuation* is an expanded treatment of much of the second half of Book V— a section which, structurally, had required an extremely rapid pace, causing much of what potentially could add new dimensions to the figure of Simplicius to be glossed over.[8] This includes not only his fuller portrayal under conditions of peace, but also Simplicius in his role as world traveller and, above all, a hermit.

It is probably an exaggeration to describe the *Continuation* as "an allegorical resumé of the thought-content of the Simplicissimus novel . . . a compressed variation of the whole novel."[9] Yet there is a certain amount of recapitulation of the central themes. The motif of money and wealth that receives so much emphasis in the trunk novel, especially in Book III, recurs here. First it is the main topic of discussion between Greed and Extravagance in the Hell allegory. Then it appears in a negative way: Simplicius' renunciation of it as part of his ascetic way of life. Only by means of the ruse of the nobleman in Chapter 16 do coins find their way again into Simplicius' possession when they are surreptitiously sewn into the seams of his new coat. Significantly, this is done as reward for Simplicius' discovery of hidden treasure on his host's estate. This whole episode occurs near the midpoint of the story (Ch. 16), as does the corresponding parallel event in *Simplicissimus*, Book III, Ch. 12. In the final sections of the sequel, money is again renounced, this time successfully since he has no need for it on the island. The motif is further varied by the contrast of the carpenter's folly in hoarding a treasure.

Similarly, the theme of the constant changeability of human affairs receives the main emphasis. The opening motto imme-

diately prepares us for this development: "Inconstancy alone is
constant, in joy and sorrow." The impressive figure of Baldanders
in Chapter 9 lends a new form to the theme and also provides
the major impetus for Simplicius' wanderings in the middle section of the book. The peculiar allegory of the scrap of paper
(Chs. 11 and 12) that tells its own tale of manifold transforma-
tions from the hemp-field to the trash-heap further concretizes
Baldanders' meaning for Simplicius. Thus he aptly describes
himself, near the middle of the section (Ch. 15) as "a ball thrown
about by changing fortune; an example of transformation; and
a mirror of the inconstancy of human nature." *Vanitas*, therefore,
is also the theme of the *Continuation*, but with a shift in emphasis. Here it is the folly of acquiring money, as well as inconstancy, which are placed in the foreground. Other facets of
vanitas are far less in evidence here. The egregrious sins (violence and lust), and ambition, pride, love, marriage, and learning
are not given the same resounding condemnation in Book VI as
in the novel.

There are also parallels in the composition of the two works.
Again the midpoints of sections receive the major emphasis. Here
clear-cut divisions and proportions emerge from this seemingly
meandering tale. The twenty-seven chapters were obviously conceived as a three-part unit, each subunit consisting of nine
chapters and having characteristics sharply distinct from the
other two.[10] Scholte aptly describes them as "static," "dynamic,"
and "meditative," respectively. Chapters 1 through 9 show Simplicius passively observing allegorical representations of life. The
second part, Chapters 10 through 18, is the travel narrative, and
in its restlessness corresponds to Books II and IV. Also the high
point of success (but low point of morality) occurs near the
midpoint (his possession of money and his lies), as in Book III.
The parallel with the trunk novel ceases here, however, for
Chapters 10 through 27 depict Simplicius as being relatively
safe from temptation and at an advanced stage of maturity. The
struggle between good and evil is now completely externalized
in the carpenter's torments, with Simplicius acting as a concerned onlooker, but hardly endangered himself. To be further
noted here with respect to midpoints is the fact that within each
nine-chapter division, there is an emphasis on the middle or fifth
chapter, i.e., 5, 14, and 23, for in all three an important turn of

events occurs.[11] The midpoint of the whole *Continuation,* however, remains the most emphatic, for here money, deception, and a fever combine to show Simplicius' dangerous involvement with the world he had renounced. As in Book III, this midpoint is the crest of a wave of *vanitas,* rising again in Simplicius' life, his having reentered human society with renewed hopes of joining it—if not, as before, to improve it with Utopian projects. The outcome is another completion of the cycle, a return to isolation.

But is it altogether a return? Simplicius is, of course, again a hermit at the end of the story. Yet how different this bright, tropical hermitage is from that of the sombre forests of Germany. His progress can thus be more fully described as an ascension to a corresponding but higher position on a spiral. His life is hardly "Saturnian" any more, with the relatively minor exceptions of his solitude, and his avoidance of sloth by working in his relatively unnecessary garden. Food and shelter are available with a minimum of labor. His bookish predilections are magnificently fulfilled by the "great book of the world,"[12] in which he contemplates and glorifies God's wondrous works (Ch. 23); and by his own writings. There is an atmosphere of radiant joy in the new surroundings, which is not even lacking in sensuous appeal. The severe asceticism of the former hermit has all but disappeared.

There is another major aspect of Simplicius' insular life which, so far, was totally lacking, in fact which is unique in Grimmelshausen's writings—namely, the mystical experience, described with considerable poetic skill in Chapters 24 through 26. This is introduced by the verse carved into a tree: "O highest of all Good! Thou dwellest in such a way in the dark light / That for the great clarity, we cannot see the vast splendor." The sense of these cryptic lines is made manifest in the cave allegory which follows. Simplicius sits alone in pitch-darkness, alone in possession of the fire-flies (representing the word of God), while the Dutch officers and the chaplain grope helplessly in the dark.[13] Thus Grimmelshausen enters but once—however impressively—the world of Christian mysticism which rose in greatest "dark splendor" in the poems of his contemporary religious lyricists—Angelus Silesius, Catharina Regina von Greiffenberg, Andreas Gryphius, and many others.[14]

To this allegory is added a clever narrative device. For the first time since the beginning of Book I, third-person narration is substituted for the first-person point of view, for the last four chapters of the *Continuation* are narrated by the Dutch sea captain. This has a combination of effects. Foremost is the striking contrast in point of view that is created by this factual, sober Calvinist's reportage, juxtaposed with the exuberant *gloria dei* sounded in the final passage, which was written by the hermit. Secondly, Simplicius' whole being as hermit is thus fully depicted as never before, with the external view added to the interior autobiography pervaded by subjective religious experience. Not to be overlooked also is the very first physical description of him, conveying a generally pleasing impression in spite of his outlandish garb (Ch. 26). Most important is the ingenious concrete representation of the mystical experience by means of the cave episode. Finally, the sea captain's narration serves the function, both literally and symbolically, of returning Simplicius' tale to the world, by conveying the palm-leaf manuscript to Europe, as well as providing the detached viewpoint that is such a fitting final touch.[15]

The narrative artistry of the *Continuation* as a whole hardly measures up to that of the trunk novel. The tantalizing, multistructured composition of Books I through V is but weakly reflected here. The allegory dominates it to the point of occasional stagnation. The main cause for this and other instances of lack of vitality is probably that Grimmelshausen too often entered realms in which he had too little experience. The final section, however, rescues the *Continuation* from falling flat. It also expands and deepens the sketchy action and the eremitic conclusion of the final section of Book V. In the long run, at least, the serpentine, yet subtly directed path of the Pilgrim Simplicius, is worth following.

III   The Life of the Arch-Swindler and Adventuress Courage

If the *Continuation* and the next sequel, *Courage,* are read in order, as Books VI and VII of the Simplician cycle, the effect of the contrast comes close to being one of shock. Simplicius ends his tale (temporarily) in the pious serenity and mystical harmony of his insular Paradise. The life story of Courage immediately strikes the dissonant chords of the extreme turbulence of an era and life-style that made monsters out of many human beings in the Thirty Years' War. The new phase of the cycle necessitates the hero's return to civilization, in order to justify his role in Courage's story—albeit remotely—and to maintain the overall relevance to the cycle. The near-miracle the return required comes about by means of a kind of narrative legerdemain, of which the reader of the main books of the cycle is unaware; for this is all told in brief anecdotal pieces appended to the fifth edition of *Simplicissimus* (including the *Continuation*) and entitled *First, Second,* and *Third Continuation,* and *Supplement.* Here Simplicius is transported from his remote hideaway back to the world. At first he reenters the story only by means of the numerous allusions to him in *Courage,* but then he reappears in the flesh, as a member of society in *Springinsfeld.*

The unobtrusively placed series of anecdotes serves to explain how Simplicius returns to Europe: he is captured and abducted by savages, then rescued by the crew of a Portuguese ship. These brief *Continuations,* if not psychologically or logically convincing, at least tend to make the transition from Book VI to Book VII less abrupt.[16] When one considers the relationship of *Courage* to the trunk novel, rather than to the immediately preceding Book VI, however, any doubts as to its relevance to the cycle must disappear. In fact, it has come to be recognized as a counterpart, in numerous ways, to *Simplicissimus,* and as such is second only to it among its author's works, as far as fame and influence are concerned, particularly in our century through Brecht's *Mother Courage.*[17]

Courage opens the final series of four sequels in which someone other than Simplicius is the main character (although he appears or is mentioned in all of them). It also constitutes the first half of a unit formed by Books VII and VIII in which the background is predominantly the Thirty Years' War, and the main character is a picaresque figure, with great emphasis on the soldier's life, particularly its most brutal and distasteful side. Courage and Springinsfeld further develop the Satanic potentials of the trunk novel found in Olivier or, to a lesser degree, in Simplicius at his worst. Other Simplician roles—such as the benignly moralizing "fool" type, the "Robin Hood" figure (Huntsman of Soest) or the pious hermit—are altogether foreign to them.

Courage is a sequel in a complex sense. Most of its action does not chronologically follow the trunk novel. In fact, its early chapters predate Simplicius' birth. The time of its narration to a scribe occurs after the publication of *Simplicissimus*—indeed, is precipitated by it, with the intriguing motivation of revenge, on Courage's part, for Simplicius' description of her as "more *mobilis* than *nobilis*" in Book V, Chapter 6. *Courage* is, then, literature propagated by literature, and reflects and comments on its parent work, as does Part Two of *Don Quixote* on Part One. Her vindictiveness has a strangely ironical twist in that her act of revenge on Simplicius entails the total destruction of whatever may be left of her own reputation by baring the most damaging facts of her life. And this is in response to Simplicius' almost trivial attack on her "virtue," in which he did not even reveal her name. Her vengeful motivation does, however, serve immediately to set the tone of rage accompanying the narration of her frustrated past. Also the fact that her hatred and anger are here directed against one of the many men who caused her unhappiness underscores a major factor in her emotional development as a woman. On the psychological level, the work is a tirade of a profoundly injured woman against men.

As in *Simplicissimus*, Grimmelshausen worded the title and subtitle of the book with obvious care and fullness in order to indicate *in nuce* the entire theme and structure of the tale:

Spite Simplex or the detailed and wondrously strange life history of the archfraud and runagate Courage, how she first was the wife of a captain of horse, afterwards the wife of a captain of infantry, further the wife of a lieutenant, presently the wife of a sutler, the wife of a musketeer, and finally the wife of a gypsy. Expertly carried out, and excellently described, and just as entertaining, agreeable and profitable to contemplate as Simplicissimus himself. All of it dictated by the person of Courage herself for the displeasure and disgust of the well-known Simplicissimus.[18]

The three references to Simplicissimus suggest more than sufficient relevance to the trunk novel.

The subtitle of the work presents a different kind of sequence from that appearing on the title page of *Simplicissimus*. In the latter, a cyclic form was indicated, whereas Courage's tale is described as an episodic sequence of events all connected with marriages. Such a progression being a characteristic trait of the rogue's novel, the question arises as to what extent Courage is a *pícara.* This feminine counterpart to the tradition of *Lazarillo de Tormes* was definitely known in seventeenth-century Germany: at least three German versions of the feminine rogue's novel (under varying titles) by Andrea Perez (the pseudonym of Francisco de Ubeda) had been published in Grimmelshausen's lifetime.[19] Comparison of this well-known narrative with *Courage,* however, immediately shows that they have little in common.[20] As far as more *general* picaresque features are present, however, it is obvious that Courage is "roguish"; is closely associated with the lower social strata (especially at the end), in spite of her noble parent; serves a large number of "masters" (i.e., husbands and lovers; as well as clients when she is a prostitute); and follows the typical meandering course through the war. Indeed, in these ways, *Courage* is more picaresque than *Simplicissimus.*

Probing more deeply into the story, we note that Grimmelshausen's own description of *Courage* indicates two important links with *Simplicissimus,* neither of which involves the picaresque novel. The first is the theme of instability, here presented in an exceptionally poignant variation, reflected in a woman's persistent and agonizing failure to achieve a lasting marriage. Her response to dissatisfaction, however, is opposite to that of Simplicius: instead of renouncing the world and its *vanitas,* and turning to God, she holds on to life with ever-growing tenacity. Secondly, the sequence of husbands, as given in the subtitle, shows a definite relevance to her ambiguous position in society. Grimmelshausen very meaningfully oversimplifies this development in the subtitle by indicating *only* a descent in the social scale, from husband to husband, thus omitting the marriage with the second infantry captain and the near-marriage with the second cavalry captain (Chs. 10 and 12, resp.), as well as the very brief union with the third infantry captain (Ch. 23). These three marriages involve *rises,* though temporary, in Courage's fortunes during the overall descent. In his summary, Grimmelshausen obviously wished to focus exclusively on the descent. Thus Courage, like Simplicius, moves about on several social levels. Simplicius' position, however, *remains* ambiguous in its constant fluctuation; whereas her fate is ultimately directed toward her permanent fall to the role of a gypsy's wife. Yet some ambiguity is present in the regal splendor with which she acts out this final role.

Unlike Simplicissimus, then, Courage undergoes a definite change in her social being—that of a woman faced by a predominantly male world and molded by her sufferings. The story as a whole is one of character formation, and thus belongs more to the realm of *Bildungsroman* than does the trunk novel. Not only is this manifest in the psychologically meaningful sequence of her love-life, but also, as in most of Grimmelshausen's writings, by emphasizing the midpoint of the story—in this case, a definite peripetia. This is found in the central—thirteenth and fourteenth —chapters (of twenty-eight altogether), where Courage falls precipitately from the life of a noblewoman (residing in the castle of the second cavalry captain) whom she is about to marry), to a condition of animallike servitude, then prostitution, then liaisons with simple soldiers. The story consists, therefore, of two clearly distinguishable halves: "in the first, she is drawn into the world's corruption as a result of her weakness, circumstances, and lack of piety; and is corrupted by worldly activities and, through depravity, herself becomes the source of further contagion. . . . She is passive. . . . Not until the second half does she become the avenger of the female sex on the male." [21] The end result of this psychological development is her "revenge" on Simplicius.

Courage has eleven important liaisons with men: (1) the first cavalry captain, (2) the first infantry captain, (3) the lieutenant, (4) the second infantry captain, (5) the second cavalry captain, (6) the cavalryman, (7) Springinsfeld, (8) the third infantry captain, (9) Simplicissimus, (10) the musketeer, and (11) the Gypsy lieutenant. At least seven of them are genuine marriages, including the common-law tie with Springinsfeld, with whom she has a written contract, even though there is no wedding ceremony. The affair with the second cavalry captain in Chapter 12 is clearly aimed at a marriage, prevented only by the interference of his parents. Also the others give rise to hopes of marriage. The time spent with the cavalryman was too brief for a marriage to ensue; his execution then permanently cuts short her hopes. No mention is made of any sanction by law or church of her last liaison with the gypsy lieutenant; but it seems likely that it is a common-law union. In other words, the novel tells a tale of frustrated but dogged attempts of a woman to find and hold her man.

To be sure, this universal feminine drive manifests itself in a highly individualized form. Her frequent lapses into prostitution and her valor and aggressiveness as an Amazon and virago type are generally regarded as deviational. Such traits have led most critics to join in chorus with Grimmelshausen's seemingly unqualified moral condemnation of her on the final page of the novel.[22] That her immorality is frequently extreme can scarcely be denied; but there has been a strange insensitivity on the part of critics toward the mitigating causes of her immorality, as well as toward other redeeming features. Grimmelshausen's sweeping moralizations at the end of a story are never designed to tell the whole truth: this is a dramatic gesture of the author as moralist stepping from the wings and speaking directly to the audience. We have seen a similar donning of the didactic mask in the long-winded trumpeting of the *vanitas* theme at the end of Book V. That this passage in *Simplicissimus* was bodily lifted from another author suggests that Grimmelshausen himself may well have had something different or additional to say along these lines, especially in view of the fact that Simplicius soon abandons his resolution to renounce the world. Such an ending, with all its moral absolutism, creates only a provisional state of affairs, and is a convenient way of ending the work, and little more. The same applies to the ending of Book V, followed soon by Simplicius' second return to the world he has renounced.

An important clue to the similarly provisional nature of the conclusion of *Courage* is that here, too, Grimmelshausen takes recourse to another author (Garzoni) for the wording of his moralizations.[23] The ending of her story is thus really not so conclusive after all. The apparent finality of this moral rigidity later dissolves into a more humanely flexible attitude, when she appears in *Springinsfeld* and *Plutus' Council-Chamber*. In the former (Chs. 4–6), she is depicted in regal splendor among her gypsy subjects. In the latter, she finally shows the full burden of her age. Though she is still a commanding figure among her subordinates, her beauty has faded completely, and she now yearns for the riches, which she now has the knowledge to acquire from men, but no longer the necessary physical appeal.[24]

There is in both cases some moralizing about her activities, past and present, but an admixture of admiration and pity is also unmistakable.

We need not, however, go beyond her autobiography to show that she is not properly described as a monstrous harlot, thief, and swindler. The most powerful mitigating factor is the "male culpability" that is the main source of her immorality.[25] Her first husband (the first cavalry captain) provides the major impetus for her bitterness against men by avoiding marriage with her until he is on his deathbed. This initial disappointment sets the stage for the Vienna episode—her first period of prostitution, into which she, still very young, is gradually lured by lascivious rich men and a clever procuress. Her third husband, the lieutenant, becomes brutal and domineering as soon as the marriage is consummated—until, that is, he is sent packing by the more formidable Courage. The fifth liaison takes her into a euphoric state as the beloved of the second cavalry captain, with whom she has a fairy-tale romance, complete with castle, until his parents put an abrupt end to it. This high point of her hopes is preceded and followed by sharply contrasting depths of misery: the rape, beatings, and obscene tortures at the hands of the soldiers beforehand, and the desperate return to prostitution in Hamburg afterwards. From this point onward, her descent in social prestige is accelerated.

This descent has its definite compensation, however, for she manages to control her own destiny somewhat better than before and to maintain a certain proud integrity by intelligently choosing men who are beneath her in abilities, and with whom she can, therefore, cope all the better. She exemplifies, in a strange way, what was apparently a prominent belief of the time—that a woman's evil and the resulting unhappiness are caused by men. She therefore learns to maintain the upper hand over them in order to stave off injury. Grimmelshausen not only implies this idea in Courage, but clearly states it in The Satirical Pilgrim.[26]

Some aesthetic matters must be considered as well. Here, too, critics have remained strangely insensitive not only to the magnetic beauty—so fully conveyed by Grimmelshausen's artistry—of this prefiguration of Manon Lescaut, but also to her impressive grandeur at certain points. The latter blossoms forth invariably when she has achieved fulfillment as the powerful and

majestic, yet feminine, woman that she is at her best. She is
such a figure during her happier unions with men—the first and
second infantry captains, the second cavalry captain, Springinsfeld (to a degree), and the gypsy lieutenant. Her marriage with
the second infantry captain is unquestionably the happiest, and
here (Chs. 10 and 11) she is in her greatest glory. It is no
accident that this marriage is preceded by the exhilarating discovery that she, like Simplicissimus, can lay some claim to noble
lineage. Consistent with her new self-esteem are the almost
pedantic contractual legalities with which she, now highborn,
prepares for her marriage at the end of Chapter 10. She also
lays the most solid possible foundation by confessing much of
her past to her fiancé, omitting only the mention of her prostitution. A welcome addition to her new household is her nurse,
whom she refers to as "mother" and treats with great tenderness. Although in the field with an army, she supervises a
household-on-wheels with loving attention in the conventionally
approved way.

Her Amazonian traits, however, move her to join in battle
with her husband, yet still for reasons consistent with her role
as wife: "To show my husband straightway from the start that my
nickname was fitting indeed, nor need he be ashamed of it. . . ." [27]
She thereby actually succeeds in winning more of his approval
than before. The marriage thrives:

The longer my husband and I were together, the fonder we grew of
each other, and each counted himself fortunate because he had the
other for a mate: and if we had not been ashamed, I believe I should
not have strayed from his side, night or day, in the trenches, on watch,
and in all engagements.

In the final days of the marriage, her simultaneously vigorous
and tender concern keeps her by his side (to remove the lice
from his body) until his death in battle. Thus she loses her
perfect mate, with whom she has had a full marriage, in which
she nonetheless has been as valiant, as much a soldier, as men,
yet remaining totally a woman in her motivations. To bring such
a character to full blossom in two chapters is one of Grimmelshausen's consummate feats as storyteller. Her hard-driving, even
violent, action is an apt expression of her passion for the man

at whose side she consistently wants to remain. How can one fail to feel compassion for her and to understand (if not condone) her desperation—especially in the ensuing vacillations of her fortune, when she is tortured and raped, then enjoys hopes of another good marriage with the second cavalry captain, then is again plunged into misery and prostitution?

Only such a sequence of demoralizing contrasts can drive her into the monstrosities of the second half of the story. Only the most extreme and sudden excesses of misfortune can contort this otherwise virtuous and lovely Amazon into the grotesque (yet still impressive) figure of a gypsy queen, swindler, and thief.

The process leading to her ultimate degradation is precipitated by the bombardment of miseries that are treacherously juxtaposed with bliss in the central Chapters 10 through 14. Henceforth, Courage desperately fortifies the innermost, tenderest woman in herself against further injury by marrying beneath her, thus making her mate, Springinsfeld, more manageable, and his future loss less painful to her. This purposeful self-degradation bestows a certain strangeness and eccentricity in her. When she enters into a detailed written marriage contract with him, we are reminded of a similar arrangement—the one with her favorite, the second infantry captain. This seems to portend success (though not necessarily longevity) for the marriage and in a peculiar way this promise is fulfilled, since the two parties accept and carry out their separate and clear roles, unusual as they may be, and vastly different from those in the other marriage. The prime difference here is that she is mistress of the household, whereas with the captain she was an equal. Furthermore, social acceptability has no bearing on the later marriage, except possibly in the proviso that the marriage would be made official should she become pregnant. She practices prostitution on the side. It is not surprising that the contract is dissolved when Springinsfeld's resentment explodes in a fit of rage, as if from subconscious depths, during his sleep.

The Springinsfeld liaison is a parody of the marriage with the second captain of infantry. It is not unlikely that at this point, the awareness of her barrenness contributes to her further transformation.[28] The parody of her former self continues in various ways. During the Springinsfeld episode, there is a series of adventures, told in anecdotelike chapters, which portray her as a picara. She plays pranks typical of this role: her vulgar revenge on the Italian courtesan and apothecary (Ch. 17), the purchase and sale of the magic flask (Ch. 18), the jewel theft (Ch. 19), and the robbery of the Italian merchants' goods (Ch. 20). Generally, these episodes are designed to arouse more admiration and interest in her cleverness than moral indignation.

After ridding herself of Springinsfeld, Courage enters a new phase that seems to offer hopes for a rise in her fortunes, as well as placing her in a more favorable light. She has repeatedly shown tender feelings for her foster mother, who now dies, and leaves Courage alone. This sets the stage for another marriage, again with an infantry captain (the third)—a rank that previously has borne promise for her. This marriage, however, is so ephemeral that it requires only a dozen lines of prose to trace it from the first meeting to his death in battle. Also in this chapter, she seems to be settling down to a stable life by purchasing a farm, but then succumbs again to prostitution and contracts syphilis. Her illness occasions her visit to the spa, where she meets Simplicius, as described in Book V, Chapter 6. This signals her final attempt to enter conventional society. After Simplicius rejects her, and she is run out of town for a sexual adventure, she settles for a musketeer as a husband, who, like the rest, is soon left dead on the battlefield.

In the final two chapters, Courage, the gypsy woman, is an outcast. Here she again plays the picara with respect to her pranks and ruses. Yet she is now also the queen of her own realm, but lives by her wits in the ambiguous picaresque way. She robs her client, whose fortune she tells, and with an ingenious ruse lures the farmers out of a village, so that some of her band are free to steal the food prepared for a church festival. A stern moral condemnation, however, is inappropriate here, for the victims almost deserve to be robbed for so stupidly allowing themselves to be tricked. And Courage and her band take on a certain exotic appeal. Later, in Chapters 4 to 6 of *Springinsfeld*, in which she appears in a highly sympathetic light as the duchess of her underworld society, this becomes all the more the case.

Thus her descent and alienation from conventional society are quite relative matters and should not lead to oversimplifications concerning her "destruction" or "degradation." In her own peculiar manner, she has maintained an impressive autonomy and integrity. She is very positively portrayed within her own world—the underworld—and remains there the shining center of her own solar system, as several times before. Her character is not destroyed, but transformed—corrupted in a moral sense, it is true, but still possessing the same enormous vital force with which she increasingly dominates her environment. This final stage of development is aptly depicted on the frontispiece of the original edition, in which she is shown in a commanding pose, mounted—though here it is with the eccentric touch of being on a mule, in contrast to her former horse mount.

It would be foolhardy to attempt to minimize the obscenity of *Courage*. Even twentieth-century critics have been driven into a prevalently moralistic tone in assessing the tale, to the detriment of its merit as a work of art. Not that these extreme qualities should be rationalized in any way into more palatable ones. Instead, it should be recognized that they are an important part of an implicit statement that the story as a whole makes: namely, that it requires the most outrageous and obscene forms of cruelty and exploitation to transform her. The process of her corruption is so emphatically and shockingly flung into the reader's face, however, that, unless his sensitivities remain delicately responsive under its bruising impact, he can easily miss the potential of a tender feminity that is so stupidly abused, yet remains perceptible almost to the end. Hers is an either-or character. Since she cannot surrender all of her vast womanly power to a husband in a conventional marriage (altogether conceivable for her in other times), she is driven to find her abode in the only place left to her—the underworld.

If there are any doubts as to Grimmelshausen's intention of presenting her in this way, the following passage from *Springinsfeld* should dispel them:

. . . behold! there approached, mounted on a mule, a splendid gypsy woman, the likes of which I had never seen nor heard. I thus could only assume that she was, if not a queen, at least an exalted duchess of all other gypsy women. She appeared to be about sixty years old. . . . She did not have pitch-black hair, like the others; it was, instead, somewhat light-colored, and was held together with a band of gold and precious stones, like a crown. . . . From her face, which still had a vigorous look about it, one could see that, in her youth, she had not been ugly. On her ears she wore a pair of gold and enamel earrings, studded with diamonds, and around her neck a string of pearls . . .

and so on in this regal manner for another half-page. The scribe narrating this (and to whom Courage dictates her story) concludes with the remark: "I can still see her thus in my imagination, whenever I desire."[29] Only in the later work, *Plutus' Council-Chamber*, is she presented in an aesthetically less favorable light, yet still as the gypsy queen. Morally, of course, she remains as dangerous as ever in these two later passages, as the scribe indicates immediately after the above quotation when he compares her with "Babylon," the archetypal harlot in *Revelations*.

In view of the wholeness of her character and story, it is remarkable that Grimmelshausen was able to integrate this sequel into the Simplician style. And *Courage* is indeed organically linked with the trunk novel, beyond the fact that it proceeds from one of its episodes. There are several major parallels. Both Simplicius' and Courage's first acquaintance with sex comes about while they are disguised in the clothing of the opposite sex. Both begin participation in the war as baggage-train followers, then gradually become combatants. Both experience an ambiguous social elevation at midpoint, associated with their "highborn" lineage that is remote from their immediate environment. Both learn of their noble origins at a relatively late period in their lives. Both end their careers alienated from their ambiguous social origins.

The last parallel, however, also includes a sharp contrast. The goal of Simplicius' withdrawal is his redemption as a Christian. Courage's path takes her to the brink of damnation and leaves her there. The didactic message, however, remains highly susceptible to being superseded by her vitality and beauty. Unlike *Simplicissimus*, *Courage* has no sophisticated multilayered structure. It is solely a sharply focussed study of character development. As such, it is unsurpassed among Grimmelshausen's works.

IV The Curious Tale of Springinsfeld

Springinsfeld ("Hop-into-the-Field") derives his name from Courage's first command to him in Chapter 16 of her story. His subservient role, expressed in this epithet, has previously figured in the Soest episode in Books II and III, and he reaches his extreme of unmanly bondage as Courage's common-law husband and servant. His biography (Book VIII), like Courage's, entails a broadening and deepening of the Simplician cycle by means of a minor figure transformed into a major one. It tells an altogether new, though thematically related tale. *Springinsfeld* and *Courage* are further interrelated by virtue of their roles as the chief male and female figures in the sequels, partly paralleling Simplicius, partly presenting meaningful contrasts with each other as well as with the hero of the trunk novel. Both are also more picaresque in a narrow sense than Simplicius. Common ground with the whole cycle is established by the poem on the title page, which again, as at the beginning of Book VI, emphatically presents the theme of Fortune's inconstancy. Finally, *Springinsfeld,* like no other book, anticipates the remaining two books of the cycle, for already in Chapter 23 there appears the bird's nest that is to become the central symbol in Books IX and X (Books I and II of *The Miraculous Bird's Nest*). Thus *Springinsfeld* interconnects the various books more than any other single book.[30]

This function makes *Springinsfeld* less readable by itself than the other sequels. In fact, on the surface it is a peculiar conglomeration. The hero's actual life-story does not begin until Chapter 10, as the first nine chapters are taken up with the seemingly unnecessary purpose of developing a "frame" story, by means of which the various parties who hear this tale are assembled. Also included in this long introductory section is the Secretary's description of Courage as a gypsy queen (cited above, p. 112 f.) and Simplicius' entertainment of his public with feats of magic. Finally, with *eight* persons bedded down together in one room for the night and having had their night's sleep, the remaining seven (!) hours of darkness are taken up with the narration of Springinsfeld's autobiography.

It is a bleak and miserable course which this man traces against the wintry-night background of the frame story. All too often the narrative deteriorates into a mere reportage of gruesome and dreary segments of the Thirty Years' War, most of which Grimmelshausen derived from contemporary chronicles.[31] One critic seeks to justify the sheer boredom (rephrased as "the dry tone of the chronicler") of these sections on the grounds of Grimmelshausen's presumed artistic intent to express stylistically "an inner impoverishment, a spiritual atrophy." [32] Even if a reader is forearmed with this justification, however, such passages are hardly made more readable, nor is their plethora of detail truly relevant to Springinsfeld's life, which, in itself, provides an often engaging story.

Yet it would be incorrect to dismiss the sequel as disorganized. Even a superficial examination of the arrangement and the numerical relationship of the chapters immediately indicates the contrary. Predominant is the triadic development, similar to that used in Book VI. This is particularly true of Chapters 1 through 9—the first third of twenty-seven chapters. This frame story is clearly subdivided into three sections of three chapters each. The first subsection (chapters 1 through 3) deals with the three main figures of the beginning: the Secretary, Simplicius, and Springinsfeld, and their "conjunction," wherein they represent Saturn, Mars and Mercury, respectively. Chapters 4 through 6, the emphatic middle part of the section, contain the impressive Courage episode. Chapters 7 through 9 focus on Simplicissimus. After this, the groupings by chapter numbers are not so clear-cut. One would expect that Chapters 10 through 18 and 19 through 27 would form a clearly discernible section, but they do not. Yet other kinds of triadic motifs appear in the last two-thirds of the novel: the tales of the wastrels in Chapter 11 are three in number, and so are Springinsfeld's wives. Grimmelshausen apparently intended to structure *Springinsfeld* triadically, but he seems to have lost sight of this plan in the course of the writing.

The numerical structure is, of course, an external shell and requires substantive support. The views regarding the content of the tale is controversial, with opinions ranging from Koschlig's —that the work is seriously disorganized, particularly in the case of the "bag-of-tricks" episodes in Chapters 7 and 8, allegedly added later for economic reasons[33]—to that of Streller,[34] who maintains that all parts of the story are integrated into a meaningful whole. The difficulty in assessing the tale lies in its double function—to focus on a single character, and to draw together various strands from the other books. A distinct separation of these two functions is helpful.

The main problem is the justification of the first nine chapters —a disproportionately lengthy introduction, which can be justified only by its contribution to the whole cycle, since relatively little of it concerns Springinsfeld himself. We first encounter the Secretary, whose importance lies almost exclusively in the fact that he narrates the whole sequel. For the first time in the cycle, Grimmelshausen here employs a narrator who is not directly involved in the events of the story (except for his encounter with Courage). Simplicius and Courage had narrated their own life-stories, as does Springinsfeld (albeit second-hand) within the frame of the Secretary's report to the reader. In the two remaining Books (IX and X), we also encounter first-person narrators who are only partially involved in the action. As the end of the cycle is approached, the trend is toward greater detachment on the part of the narrator. This goes hand in hand with a greater variety of persons and episodes, a more loosely connected narrative sequence, and a sense of surveying ever greater and more varied segments of society. Furthermore, by virtue of the Secretary's detached position, we receive, through his eyes, the first relatively objective portrayals of Simplicius, Courage, and Springinsfeld. Simplicius is now highly impressive in a new way, for he is wearing a curiously exotic garb, apparently brought home from abroad, and having more than healthy appetites. Yet he commands great respect and admiration from all those present. He wields considerable power in his own world of peasants and burghers, though often in strange ways, as with his whimsical magic tricks. In Chapters 4 through 6, Courage is also presented as an impressive figure. Springinsfeld, however, is depicted as a cantankerous old beggar, thus coloring our attitude toward his later story.

Simplicissimus himself, the main character of the ten-book novel, now reaches his final stage of development, largely in Chapters 7 through 9. He is no longer a lonely hermit, but neither the helpless toy of the world's fortune, as was often the case in the trunk novel. (He does resemble, however, the character depicted in the three short *Continuations* following Book VI). Having returned to the world, he is deeply rooted, and active, in society, yet manages to remain uncorrupted by its *vanitas*. His position is even a bit exalted, for he plays the role of lay preacher and magician. He entertains, but with a didactic aim. In Chapter 2, by converting mediocre wine into good wine, he performs a kind of eucharistic ritual to remind his audience of Christ's sacrifice. In Chapter 7, he allegorizes the message of his writings by means of the "magic" book with which one can make them appear as being empty or, depending on the individual reader's view, as having beneficial moral content. Finally, in his role as soul-saver, he is instrumental in securing Springinsfeld's possible future salvation. At the beginning of Chapter 7, he has also expressed hopes—however slim they may seem—for Courage's future redemption. Thus Simplicius' ultimate mission is not the glorification of God in solitude, as it seems to be at the conclusions of both Books V and VI, but rather one of service as a kind of informal lay preacher, philosopher, and entertainer. Simplicius continues primarily in these functions throughout the remainder of the cycle, whose overall purpose also remains true to his new mission: to point out sin and folly, and to redirect his listeners toward righteousness and ultimate redemption, however egregious their past wrongdoings may have been.

Springinsfeld's tale traces precisely such a process, amidst all the digressions mentioned above. Like Courage, he bears definite picaresque features. The adventurous and the exotic elements are accented from the start by his family background—he is the offspring of a Greek noblewoman and an Albanian juggler and tightrope walker. His roguish pranks, his adventurous career as a soldier, and his relatively subordinate station further suggest the amoral, yet likable picaro. And such features are, indeed, present in the three initial anecdotes of Chapter 11, centering on sharp rises and falls in a soldier's fortunes. Yet these little tales have an altogether different potential. Designed largely to be amusing, they also touch upon a few main themes. The folly of a rogue turned rich man overnight can easily deteriorate into the ruthlessness of the miser. Springinsfeld does not remain a predominantly comical figure, but turns more and more into the disgusting scoundrel. Picaresque pranks give way to malicious mischief, and even to outright savagery.

During the war, Springinsfeld engages in far more actual combat than either Simplicissimus or Courage. The high point (or low point) in his military career is the sickening murder of a helplessly wounded officer on the battlefield. The act is committed and narrated with the callousness of an experienced soldier interested primarily in booty. Though not really a coward, Springinsfeld is the very antithesis of the gallant *miles christianus*, a type briefly represented by Hertzbruder in Book V. His greed is also closely related to his three ill-fated marriages. All three wives are uncommonly bent on acquiring wealth: Courage as a sutler and prostitute, the second spouse as an innkeeper's wife, and the minstrel-girl by means of various forms of entertainment and charlatanry. Thus the vice of greed, present in Simplicius as the Huntsman of Soest, is made thoroughly despicable in *Springinsfeld*.

The result is the inwardly impoverished life that is Springinsfeld's, in the course of which, however, there are usually ample supplies of money and possessions to be had, even when he is an aged beggar, whose apparent helplessness is a mere ruse to obtain alms. He is isolated in the cold, bleak, fearsomely hostile world that reflects his inner self. A full symbolic representation of this world is found in the masterfully conceived episode of Chapters 16 and 17, where Springinsfeld must take refuge overnight on a rooftop, in the dead of winter, with snarling wolves threatening to devour him if he descends. Later another pack of wolves turns out to be actually tormenting devils from Hell (*Miraculous Bird's Nest*, Part I, Ch. 20). The hellish overtones of the scene and of Springinsfeld's life in general seem likewise to be conveyed here. This episode in which he is called to account for his deeds can also be viewed as representative of the ruthless soldier's experience in the Thirty Years' War. Then, as always, it was possible to come face-to-face with Hell in war. Gryphius' sonnet "Hell" ("Die Hölle") is further testimony to this awesome reality emerging from direct experience with war. Grimmelshausen's Hell, however, is a frozen one, like the Cocytus of Dante's *Commedia*. The cold, dark atmosphere of the frame story and much of the main body of the tale is an effective preparation for, and reinforcement of, the wintry wolfpack episode.

The extreme nature of Springinsfeld's evil has its point in its relevance to the moral lesson: namely, that even the very worst individuals still have a chance of redemption. On the very last page of the book, it is expressly stated that, in all probability, Springinsfeld is not doomed to eternal damnation. Immediately before his death, he has "recast himself into a totally new man, and was prevailed upon to lead a Christian and better way of life. . . ." Looking back on the story, one finds that this is no abrupt turn of events. Toward the end, definite hopes for Springinsfeld's moral regeneration are expressed. As early as Chapter 14, he shows clear awareness of the inescapable folly of the soldier's life.[35] At the end of Chapter 23, he attempts to persuade his third wife to make a more honest living than thieving with the aid of the miraculous bird's nest. In the following chapter, he is horrified by her lack of scruples. These seeds of moral regeneration are brought to fruition by Simplicius.

Again, as in Books I thorugh VI, the serpentine course is ultimately directed toward religious salvation. This is the most basic sense in which Springinsfeld's tale resembles that of Simplicius. *Springinsfeld* thus brings the progress of the ten-book narrative to the point where the three major figures' final stages of development are reached. The cycle can now progress to a new and more encompassing realm.

At this point, a brief digression is necessary in order to discuss *Plutus' Council-Chamber,* which is not a part of the ten-book cycle, but is clearly an offshoot of *Springinsfeld,* and of considerable interest in connection with it as well as with the whole Simplician world. This companion piece offers a particularly revealing study in its *contrasts* with *Springinsfeld. Plutus' Council-Chamber* shares with *Springinsfeld* the fact that, again, Simplicius and members of his family assemble with other persons who, on this occasion, are partly of higher social rank, including even powerful members of the nobility. The main external difference from *Springinsfeld* is that the work consists almost wholly of dialogue, conducted according to the rules of politeness and elegance appropriate in the presence of nobles.[36] Furthermore, the atmosphere is that of a peaceful summer setting, in sharp contrast with that of war and winter which dominates *Springinsfeld.* The company assembles by chance in a small valley near the spa of Peterstal, where all is cheerful and serene, the natural beauty of summer being enhanced by the unmistakable sign of peace and prosperity—the abundance of food and drink.

A single topic is discussed throughout: money. The problems

of wealth, ranging from its corruption in superfluity to its painful lack, have been raised many times before by Grimmelshausen, particularly in Books III and IV of *Simplicissimus*. A number of his contemporaries also wrote works on this subject, and he may owe a great deal to them.[37] Despite the extent of these derivations, no minor *Simplicianum* is so characteristic of the matured Simplicissimus as this one, written four years before its author's death. The hero is still primarily the didactic satirist, but without the frequent severity and gloom of former times. He is introduced with delightful whimsy as part of the company finds him in the woods playing to himself on a gigantic *trompet de marin* or *tromba marina*.[38] As the formal dialogue ensues, the theme of wealth having been ceremoniously chosen, the characters are sharply typified in their various attitudes toward money. It becomes more and more apparent that the problems touched upon are labyrinthine and probably insoluble. Simplicius takes full advantage of this situation by cleverly, but cheerfully, interjecting remarks that are confusing rather than clarifying. The upshot is a lengthy display of buffoonery at the end, in which he instructs Secundatus, the ranking nobleman of the group, as to how he can virtuously rid himself of his seemingly unlimited wealth by means of various forms of outrageous extravagance.

Thus Simplicius, in spite of his burgher status, reigns supreme because of his mature wisdom, particularly when pointing out folly, even that committed by those having a much higher social standing than he himself. In his potential influence on society as a whole, he is raised to an even higher level than that attained in Chapter 7 through 9 of *Springinsfeld*.

Courage and Springinsfeld also reappear, and participate in the conversation, mainly as negative moral examples, as in Books VII and VIII; but they are treated with less severity than they were in their biographies. Simplicius is now far less personally involved in the particular sins and follies in question than he was previously. Thus the way is paved for the even more detached, but still satirical, point of view in the writings of Grimmelshausen's last few years.

V   The Miraculous Bird's Nest

Books IX and X of our ten-book novel (or Parts One and Two of the *Bird's Nest*) present special difficulties in analysis and interpretation, for they clearly constitute an anomaly within the Simplician cycle. From the outset, the reader of the whole novel must be impressed, perhaps confused, by their seeming lack of relevance to the characters of the other books. The two bearers of the miraculous nest, which, like Gyges's ring, makes them invisible witnesses of otherwise unseen events, play very minor roles in *Springinsfeld*, and have no further connection with the Simplician characters, with the exception of one episode in Chapters 14 and 15 of Part One.[39] The particular religious-didactic lessons of the two Parts, though not totally irrelevant to Books I through VIII, have not previously been emphasized. They are, simply expressed, God's ubiquity (Part One), and the peril constituted by Satan's temptations (Part Two). Further-more, their supposed incoherence has led two scholarly authori-ties to view the work as a loose sequence of more or less inde-pendent short narratives.[40] This would suggest that Grimmels-hausen ended his stupendous ten-book novel with a whimper.

The author himself flatly states in the preface to Part Two that *The Miraculous Bird's Nest* forms an indispensable part of the total Simplician work, to the extent that the whole cannot be properly understood without it. The interrelationship is bolstered by a reference to the two religious-didactic lessons. As for the difficult matter of its genre and structure, it would follow that if the work is externally linked to the other eight books, it was conceived to have some internal coherence—if, that is, we are to take Grimmelshausen's remarks seriously, and there is no reason for not doing so. Furthermore, the author points out that he has employed the same satirical style as in the other Sim-plician writings, so that the otherwise bitter pill of didacticism is coated with sugar of entertaining narrative. Although pleasur-able to read, each of the two parts of the *Bird's Nest* is a little "tract" (*Traktätlein*), as he calls them repeatedly in the prefaces of Part Two.

It may, however, be doing the expert storyteller Grimmels-hausen a great injustice to view the conclusion of his *magnum opus* as a pearly string of sugar-coated pills, loosely connected by the one common feature of the bird's nest. He has previously shown himself capable of far more than this. And an essential artistic unity can, indeed, be sought—and found—elsewhere.

First one should consider the two main characters and bearers of the nest, Michael Rechulin von Sehmsdorff and the unnamed merchant side by side. The principal reason for having two bearers rather than one is indicated in Chapter 20 of Part One, where Michael weighs the possibility of the nest's falling into the hands of a man wielding great power in society, in which case its abuse could be even greater than when possessed by him, a simple man with no wealth or authority. His fear materializes when the extremely wealthy merchant becomes its master at the end of Part One, and proceeds to commit far greater wrongdoings with it than Michael had. There is, then, a progression from Part One to Part Two, from lesser to greater moral corruption inherent in the nest. This parallels the shift in emphasis from God's omnipresence to Satan's. At the same time, two different levels of society are represented by the two bearers, and a microcosmic view of society as a whole is approached. As will be seen, society, as a tangible entity, takes on far greater dimensions than before in the Simplician cycle.

The two different bearers provide central, but invisible, observation posts from which to view a vast variety of human beings. As Grimmelshausen employs the first-person narrative technique, the bird's nest and its magic power by no means provide the only common denominator for the various episodes, for the narrator's point of view is a highly unifying factor.[41] Even when Grimmelshausen derives an episode almost verbatim from another author (as he often does), he integrates it into his own creation by injecting the nest-bearer's attitudes and actions into it. One of the best examples of this is the episode concerning the students in Chapter 8 of Part One, in which the narrator becomes an instrument of a kind of justice by means of which the unseen wrong (in this case, murder) is shown to be just as subject to punishment as a crime brought before the court.[42] By analogy with the narrator, we derive from this the lesson to be learned from all of Part One: God's omnipresence.

With few exceptions, Michael is exclusively the observer. Only occasionally does he provide a warning voice or helping hand to those supposedly sinning in secrecy. The merchant, on the other hand, eagerly joins the activities of the people he observes and hopelessly embroils himself—with the impunity of secrecy, so he thinks—in those very situations against which Part One so sternly warns. Again the negative moral example follows the positive one—just as *Courage* and *Springinsfeld* follow the pious example presented in the hermit figure of Book VI. These contrasts, however, do not prevent the author from emphatically playing up the theme of the redemption of the supposedly lost sinner, as he has done at the end of each book from V on.

With other parts of the ten-book novel the *Bird's Nest* also shares a set of interrelated ideas concerning the nature of the Simplician world, which are emblematically shown on the frontispieces of both parts, and probably were drawn by Grimmelshausen himself.[43] The whimsicality of the illustration for Part One is surpassed only by that introducing *Simplicissimus*. It shows a cherublike child attempting in vain to view "the world" through a telescope; but a pile of masks before him obstructs the view. The world, represented by a globe propelled by legs, is following a serpentine path, and apparently adds to the child's difficulty in sighting it by being constantly in motion. Much taller—and therefore having a better view—stands a satyr, peering through a bird's nest and holding a mask behind his back. The latter figure is a favorite pictorial device of the satirist. (It will be recalled that both the satyr and the masks are prominent figures of the *Simplicissimus* frontispiece.) Beneath the illustration are these words:

> I contemplate, through a bird's nest, the tortuous paths pursued by the world,
> Which, however, the child cannot see through the telescope,
> For the view is blocked by masks.
> I show therewith the reason why we wander on so blindly.
> I cry "You who err, stand still,"
> And I warn each and everyone to beware of harm
> When he wishes to follow.

Thus the satyr represents the author, and the child stands for other human beings—especially the reader—to whom the illusory and inconstant nature of the world is to be revealed. Such attributes of the world as *vanitas* have been implicit before, but never singled out and dwelt upon. The danger created by false impression is particularly strongly emphasized, as in the illustrations to the fifth edition of *Simplicissimus*. There is an important connection here. In Chapter 11 of Part One Michael points out that the Elder Simplicissimus has provided his illustrations with the motto, "Der Wahn betreügt" ("Illusion deceives").[44] Thus *The Bird's Nest* and *Simplicissimus* are thematically linked.

The frontispiece of Part Two is not so rich in meaning as that of Part One. It merely represents the conjuration scene in which the merchant acquires the bird's nest. The magic circle in which he and the sorcerer are standing foreshadows subsequent warnings against the forbidden arts. The fantastic creature at which the sorcerer is waving his wand tantalizes us with the sensuous face of a beautiful woman, but spells danger in its loathsome serpent's body—a variation on traditional representations of sin. This is, in other words, yet another form of the theme of Satanic temptations, previously developed in the Olivier episodes in the trunk novel, as well as in *Courage* and *Springinsfeld*.

There are, then, a few emphatic indications pointing to the cohesiveness of *The Miraculous Bird's Nest*, to meaningful interrelationships between the two parts, and to its relevance to the ten-book novel—in spite of definite impressions to the contrary that we may have at first. The following analysis is designed to reveal, in detail, the threads of unity and the manner of their interweaving with each other and with the entire ten-book novel.

As was shown above, Grimmelshausen took special pains with the frontispiece of Part One. Here more of the essence of this Part is concentrated than on any other single page in the book. The function of the nest is quite apparent: it is the lens through which the bearer perceives reality, as opposed to the masks of deception through which the naive child is trying to look. The nest is the common denominator in almost all of the episodes. No hint is offered, however, as to *how* the story, or stories, are to be told. The figure of the spindly-legged world, however, does represent the narrative course of the work. The path it follows is clearly marked behind him in the form of a carefully drawn zigzag line. Could it be that such a simple figure provides a way to the principle underlying the order of events in the work to follow? Apparently it does, and from the very start. The first major episodes offer clear initial examples. Chapter 2 and the beginning of Chapter 3 tell the tale of an impoverished nobleman's visit to a castle, where he hopes to improve his fortunes by marrying the daughter of the owner. An amusing double irony in the situation soon develops, for the owners are as impoverished as he, and equally bent on creating the impression of wealth in order to make a rich catch. Thus both parties are wearing "masks," as in the frontispiece. So eager are the mother and daughter to capture Sir Neediness ("Herr von Drftgkt") in marriage that they are not even repelled by his habit of shrieking loudly at night in his sleep and thereupon befouling his bed! Michael does not wait to learn the outcome, for he—also ironically—decides to wander on in search of an opportunity to acquire money with the aid of the nest that makes him invisible. He does not, as later, derive the moral lesson the experience could teach him—the vanity of seeking wealth. The danger of forming a marriage on the basis of lies, however, does impress him. He moralizes on this point not only with respect to the undermining of marriage, but also of other human relationships.[45]

The abruptness of the nest-bearer's departure from the castle is accentuated by the contrast between the nobles of the first episode and the beggars of the second. This contrast is meaningful and complex. For from the first moment on, the beggars convey a sense of joy and freedom. Moreover, in spite of their profession, they are well-supplied with material wealth, including money. Thus, the course of the world in which Michael wanders, not only takes him along zigzagging paths from the high to the low in society's hierarchy; it also reveals itself as a *verkehrte Welt*, a "topsy-turvy world," full of unexpected and absurd reversals. By means of the bird's nest, the mask of wealth is removed from impoverished nobility, and the mask of poverty from the lowly. The notion that nobles are happy and free, and beggars miserable and enslaved to poverty, is also turned upside down. As human beings capable of coping with life by means of intelligence and direct action, the beggars are far superior to their social betters, as is illustrated by a series of witty anecdotes about them. This harks back to Grimmelshausen's guarded admiration for the underground society as depicted in Courage's story, particularly when she is a gypsy queen. Such sentiments probably derive from the picaresque tradition.

Michael's sympathy with the beggars is not so great, however, as to cause him to join them. Instead, the story (along with his attitudes) veers off in a new direction. He leaves the group to enjoy its spoils and freedom in order to accompany two Capuchins travelling by foot. Thus we have a transition from the worldly to the religious. The theme of religion had been introduced in the beggar episode, in which the beggars reveal their skill in feigning belief in the three major Christian denominations. Now, in Chapter 4, the main theme becomes Christianity. At first the implications thereof for daily life come under scrutiny. As Michael, in his invisible state, walks silently alongside the two uncommunicative clerics, he ponders his experience with the beggars and decides that these men should be put to use for the good of the nation by pressing them into gainful and useful employment—something far more pleasing to God than their present harmful and unproductive occupations. Thus he rejects much, if not most, of the state of affairs in which society found itself in mid-seventeenth-century Germany, for he finds both top and bottom to be behaving mainly in ways opposite to their proper functions. Indeed, they are depicted as downright parasites.[46]

The Capuchins, however, offer no solutions in their silence, and the first actual event in the chapter is by no means designed to elicit confidence in the clergy. The Capuchins are invited by a village pastor's wife to enter her house for food and drink while her husband is absent. They decline the offer, but not without the narrator's expression of doubts whether any of the three could resist the temptations of the flesh posed by the situation. Thus are introduced the themes of adultery and fornication which receive great attention throughout both Parts of *The Miraculous Bird's Nest*.

This brief event provides an introduction to the main part of the chapter, in which a more serious religious issue, that of denominational strife, is raised. The scene takes place in an inn, where the narrator, having left the Capuchins, observes a confrontation between Catholics and Calvinists. This consists of a not altogether unfriendly exchange of anecdotes about religion, most of which are designed merely to pique, but slightly, the members of the other denomination. The undercurrent of irritation threatens to surface when a Calvinist insults the Virgin

Mary. The invisible Michael steps in to punish him by knocking him down. Apparently those present are more interested in entertaining themselves and humiliating each other than in the genuine issues of the faiths they represent. This is corrected for the moment by Michael's expressly playing the role of God's instrument of punishment. In referring to his action, Michael modestly relates: "I . . . considered it God's punishment, because God is accustomed to speak the truth through sinners and generally to punish his most powerful and defiant enemies by means of the most wretched and lowly insects." [47] ("Insects," incidentally, will come to plague sinners again.) The conclusion to be drawn from this chapter is that clergy and communicants of the Christian faith alike are in no position to improve the state of the world. Only the invisible nest-bearer, though a sinner himself, recognizes the truth and acts upon it, in a manner consistent with God's will. (This is the first of a series of punishments he inflicts on sinners.) The potential self-pride involved in all this becomes no issue—with one possible subsequent exception—as it well could. The groundwork thus laid, showing the ineffectiveness of both shepherds and flocks in the Christian churches, the nest-bearer's course wanders on from one character type in Christian society to another who are engaged in various forms of folly and sin.

The next episode (Chapter 5) illustrates the unfortunate consequences of a miserly peasant's refusal to let his daughter marry, since he wishes to keep her in servitude to himself: she secretly commits fornication at night. Michael is the secret witness. But lest it be thought that peasants, with their modest means, are the only ones guilty of greed, in the next chapter the plot veers sharply again, and more highly-placed persons are depicted as callous schemers and vultures, waiting for a man to die, thereby releasing his young wife and his property for their own use.

Greed is once more touched upon at the beginning of Chapter 7, when Michael stops at an inn to quench his thirst, only to be served the watered and inferior wine of the unscrupulous innkeeper. The main event of this chapter—the attempted seduction of a girl by a clergyman—shifts the attention again to a combination of previously sounded themes: the inadequacy of the clergy, and fornication. For the second time, Michael intercedes as God's punishing agent, and carries the man outside, dumping him in the filth of the barnyard. (Michael himself later suffers the same indignity.) The action is accompanied by appropriate moralizations. The next step, however, is a curious one, not altogether consistent with Michael's role as hitherto developed. While he is attempting to leave the cellar, where he has been partaking of the clergyman's wine, an invisible spirit pushes him down the stars, as he himself later punishes a burglar. His explanation to himself—that this was a warning not to offend a clergyman again—leaves some doubt, otherwise unvoiced in the story, as to the justice of Michael's function. To this one can say only that God moves in mysterious ways, indeed.

Chapter 8 develops the religious theme in an altogether new way. As Michael accompanies two university students on their journey, he listens to a learned disputation about the existence or nonexistence of the pre-Adamites. The sterile dryness of their thinking is apparent enough in the debate itself; but it also receives more than adequate commentary in the events that follow. For as they think they are about to die at the hands of highway robbers, one of them says: "If only we had learned—instead of mere foolish things, vain musings, and silly disputations—how we should die well and blissfully." [48] Michael, however, intercedes for the second time to prevent murder, only to place the students in a position to slaughter one of the thieves, an act he prevents as well. Thus, for the second time, crimes of violence enter the story, and are soon reintroduced.

Michael's serpentine course then returns to the more familiar territory of human society and its foibles. The brief Chapter 9 is a comical interlude, juxtaposed with the deadly seriousness of the preceding and following happenings. Here a genre picture of a village wedding culminates in a seduction scene on the straw of a stable. All the previous stern moralizations about fornication are counterbalanced by the comedy of the couple's rhythmically repeated words to match their action. For the third time, Michael puts a stop to such proceedings—but unintentionally, with his laughter, thus frightening the bewildered boy and girl away. Not the remotest suggestion of a moralization accompanies this scene, and Michael is able to sleep peacefully on the straw during the night.

The events of Chapters 10 and 11 are closely interrelated,

at the same time providing a sequence of "central" importance in the special structural sense previously explained. Like Chapters 2 and 3, the episodes juxtapose extreme contrasts, but this time even greater ones than before. None of the ambiguity brought about by the nobles' poverty and misery and the beggars' wealth and happiness is now present. In great detail Grimmelshausen portrays, in Chapter 10, the affluence of a household that is so meticulously kept and filled with knickknacks that Michael senses an unreality about it, as if it were a doll's house or a painting. These characteristics are heightened by preparations for a banquet about to be held in honor of a promising suitor for the exceptionally lovely daughter. Michael's unforeseen role here is to dampen the spirits of the young lady by unintentionally showing himself to her through a mirror as she is adorning herself and rehearses gestures and facial expressions. Unknown to him, the nest does not make his mirror image invisible. Her immediate interpretation of the incident is that she is being punished for her "arrogance and folly." The effect is a partial moral improvement, for at the banquet she does not employ the feminine wiles that she had rehearsed before the mirror. Michael, however, thoroughly enjoys the food and drink, and even acquires two gold coins intended for the musician—his rationalization being that so much superabundance justifies a relatively petty theft. Besides, one of the coins finds its way into the hands of the poor family portrayed in the next chapter.

The contrasting effect of the poverty of the family of ten portrayed in Chapter 11 is one of the most purposeful juxtapositions in the whole tale, and Michael makes repeated comparisons between the two scenes to drive home the point. Not nearly as obvious is the function of the two episodes in Part One of the *Bird's Nest* as a whole. At the end of Chapter 11, Michael muses that it is God's will to challenge the rich to be humble and beneficent, and the poor to be patient and content.[49] He still finds it puzzling, however, that in carrying out the divine purpose, he appears as a devil to the wealthy lady, and as an angel to the paupers. This leads to a more general awareness of man's frequent susceptibility to illusions, even more heavily underscored by the mentioning of the motto, "Illusion deceives," in the illustrations to the fifth edition of *Simplicissimus*. Thus what is probably the strongest single link is established between *The Miraculous Bird's Nest* and the trunk novel.

These two chapters exemplify most clearly, of any section of the book, the two main features of the world as depicted in the frontispiece and to be developed in the story. It is, above all, an illusory world; and contemplating its course requires following a serpentine path, the sharp transition from wealth to poverty being its best illustration. Thus it is probably true that this section, particularly the moralizing passage ending Chapter 11, is the "center" of the work in the multiple sense already indicated for all other books in the ten-book novel.[50]

The next episode is lengthy and complex. Its main part is Michael's thwarting of a burglary attempted by the two robbers already encountered in the episode of the two contentious students. This is preceded, however, by the incidents, told with a certain lightness, involved in the theft of a cow, and later of a coat and of food. A more serious turn is taken when Michael overhears the two thieves planning the burglary. Then another contrasting section, dominated by good-natured levity, follows when Michael observes a happy bedroom scene between man and wife (the only one of its kind in the book!), then another one between their servants. The wife is making preparations to attend a wedding. Thus there is a form of dramatic irony present in these scenes, inasmuch as Michael and the reader are aware of the danger in which these blissfully unsuspecting targets of the murderous thieves find themselves. The entrance of the criminal into the house, and Michael's prevention of the burglary, constitute a highpoint with respect to brutality and bloodiness. Again, as in the two previous episodes and in Chapters 2 and 3, a scene achieves its effect by means of stark contrasts. This time, however, it is that of apparent blissful security and the real danger of violence. He manages, of course, to ward off the worst possible outcome. To be noted, finally, is another touch of potential guilt that Michael acquires in being instrumental in the sudden death of an evil man who has no opportunity for redemption. His compunction, however, is easily rationalized away upon considering that he has saved the lives of the owner of the house and his servant.

Chapter 13 consists of a series of anecdotes and musings on the subject of theft, leading both into the monastery and into

the Simplicissimus episodes of Chapters 14 and 15. Michael
gains ever deeper insights, which point to the desirability of his
own moral conversion, and the sinfulness of his past and present
life. The sequence begins with a resolution not to rob a Christian,
but to choose a Jew instead as his victim! (The latter idea is
subsequently abandoned as sinful.) A shepherd's misappropria-
tion of his master's sheep, witnessed and condemned by Michael,
presents the first variation on the theme. A shortage of food then
leads Michael into the temptation to steal, but he manages to
soothe his conscience by leaving a shoe behind in the place of
a ham, thereby "paying" for it. Further consolation comes when
the victim of the theft regards the incident as a sign from above
to repent and be reborn. His satisfaction soon evaporates, however, with the recognition that the ham was not taken for a
good purpose, and that no adequate compensation was made
for it. He is warned by an invasion of lice into his garments—
a method of punishing wrongdoing, as was indicated in Chapter
4. Not only is his soul in jeopardy, but also his body—the
latter danger being recognized upon pondering the possibility of
his being apprehended by the secular authorities, tortured and
executed as a sorcerer. An important step has thus been taken
toward Michael's moral regeneration at the end.

There are, however, several more experiences and stages before this can come about. Again the complex of themes relating
to Christianity is taken up and varied in a new way. Chapter 14
is set in a monastery, where Michael goes in the hope of acquiring a new pair of shoes. He finds the place lavishly supplied
with everything—a condition leading later to his conclusion that
the spiritual brothers were living in far too worldly a manner.
This is corroborated by the first conversation he overhears and
in which it is revealed that there has been at least one recent
instance of carousing within the monastery walls. This offense
against the dignity of the place is heightened by a malicious
plot against Simplicius the Younger, who is residing there and
whom the offending brothers think to be the person who reported
their misbehavior to the abbot. Their success in causing the
young man's dismissal, on the grounds of suspected theft, leaves
intact the mask of holiness, through which the nest-bearer has
been able to peer into the true state of affairs. Thus the way to
salvation for Michael can hardly be through the clergy. Other

representations of the clergy support this guardedly expressed idea. One is led to wonder here about the extent to which Grimmelshausen was converted from the Lutheran to the Catholic faith! The necessity of the Christian to follow the inner road of conscience alone is strongly argued here by implication.

The above episode and its sequel are separated by a short incident that dispenses with the murderous burglar who had escaped in Chapter 12. At the beginning of Chapter 15 he is apprehended and hanged for theft. Along with him thievery as a main theme and concern in the story disappears. It has been made clear that Michael must eventually desist from similar activities (which, apparently, he manages to do at the end of the story). Now the story focusses intensely on adultery and fornication. The first instance is the episode in which Simplicius and an innkeeper's wife are falsely accused of committing the act. This incident parallels the manipulated accusation of theft to which young Simplicius has been subjected at the monastery. The main difference is that, this time, Michael manages to rescue the young man when brought before the authorities.

There follows a lengthy passage, taking up the remainder of Chapter 15, which is controversial with respect to its function, if any, in the story as whole. For here Grimmelshausen is definitely engaging in literary polemics occasioned by the appearance of Phillip von Zesen's novel, *Assenat*, in which Grimmelshausen's novel on the same Old Testament theme, *The Chaste Joseph*, is attacked and allegedly plagiarized. The details of the lengthy discussion have little relevance here. It should be pointed out that, in a general way, the passage is consistent with its context, in that it deals with a form of theft—that is, plagiarism. Furthermore, by presenting Simplicissimus and his son at some length, the author strengthens the connection of this seemingly irrelevant work with the ten-book novel. Finally, an unmasking process takes place here in at least two senses: the plagiarizer, Zesen, is revealed; and the older Simplicissimus— the author's fictitious self-image—states that he himself is the author of *The Chase Joseph*; thus, although not totally unmasking him, he, at least, brings the reader one step closer to the real man behind the pseudonyms.[51] Yet, one must recognize that, thematically, the specific choice of Simplicissimus' feud with

Zesen is less compelling than most of the other ingredients of the work.

The last incident of the chapter—the failure to achieve a position for Simplicius the Younger at court because of the monastery incident—puts the finishing touches to the exposé of the monastic life. It is suggested that both the monastery and the court are cut out of the same cloth; hence Simplicius is advised to become a soldier. In this way, a possible new Simplicissimus novel about the son is projected into the future.

As Michael wanders on, the theme of fornication is resumed. Another turning point in Michael's moral regeneration is reached when he witnesses the stopping of a seduction scene between a peasant boy and girl—not by Michael himself, but as a result of the boy's sudden heeding of his conscience, which tells him that the deed cannot really be committed in secret, since God is watching them. The moral discourse which follows is topped off by a second seduction scene witnessed secretly by Michael, in which his righteous indignation over the adulterous act is aroused to the extent that he unceremoniously drags the male party off by the legs.

Yet Michael is not quite prepared for a total moral conversion. The several adventures that follow interweave all previous themes pertaining to wrongdoing and add a few new ones. The next scene, at the beginning of Chapter 17, portrays a secretly witnessed act of bribery. Michael fails to rectify the matter, however, because of the ambiguous nature of the guilt of all parties concerned. This leads him to the important conclusion that it really is not his proper role—in fact, it is not even feasible —to correct and punish the world's folly and sin. He hopes that the sinners will themselves find their own way to innocence. Another important revelation in his musings is that excusing sins in one's own mind is, in itself, a sin. That he is not yet ready to apply these newfound principles is dramatically shown when, in the next breath, he tells of stealing a loaf of bread.

A further variety of dishonesty is introduced in Chapter 18, where the sin under attack is lying—more specifically, the telling of tall tales. Its amusement value, stemming from anecdotes narrated by a hopeless Baron Münchhausen type, provides a contrast with the more serious passages of the chapter. This is particularly true of the incident that concludes Chapter 18:

Michael's own seduction of a girl, befuddled from wine, during the night following a village wedding.

The full extent of his remorse over the deed comes about only after another incident, at the beginning of Chapter 19. Here he chances upon a herdsman who is about to commit sodomy, but is prevented by Michael with his warning voice under the cloak of his invisibility, and is admonished to take the matter to the confessional. Although this time Michael is successful in his role as God's instrument, his despair over his own recent sin is extreme, in view of the irony that he finds in his holier-than-thou treatment of the herdsman. The incident, one must admit, is well designed for the sake of its shock effect in counteracting sexual misbehavior by identifying it with sexual aberration. Michael is finally ready for his conversion, which comes about as a result of contemplating nature in a manner characteristic of the time, that is, as "God's emblembook."[52] A similar scene has already occurred, in Book VI, with the same function of revealing the way to the Christian's salvation and bliss. As Michael sits meditating under a tree, at the beginning of Chapter 20, the first emblematic sign he sees is a snake pursuing, then devouring, a toad. This is a warning to him that unredeemed sinful acts and habits of human beings, represented by the toad, can be punished by being turned over to a hellish dragon, represented by the snake. Not only is Michael keenly aware of the spiritual peril in which he finds himself; but there is also a foreboding of the more weighty sins and greater punishments in Part Two. The nightingale, a contrasting figure, then sings the praise of God's glory—one of the most common literary devices of the time, familiar especially from the hermit's song in Chapter 7 of Book I of *Simplicissimus*. Michael is faced with an either-or choice in these signs found in the "Great Book of Nature."

Subsequently, Grimmelshausen employs animal emblems in an ingenious way, in that he lets them play parts, with appropriate meanings, in the remainder of this last chapter of Part One. First there is the most impressive scene of the sequence—Michael's "punishment" by a swarm of bees, which drive him into a filthy puddle, in which he can gain some relief from the stings. The emblematic import of these bees is apparent not only from the scene and context itself, but also from two previous allusions to insects as instruments of divine retribution.[53] The punishment of being immersed in filth, of course, is foreshadowed by Michael's subjecting the clergyman to the same indignity in Chapter 7. This last warning is the most effective one, for Michael now makes the crucial decision to destroy the nest.

Three more categories of emblematic creatures have yet to enter the story, however, and their meanings are not so clear-cut in their impact on Michael's future. First there enters a colony of ants near the place where Michael has torn the bird's nest into "1700 pieces." He is thereby reminded of Solomon's admonition to renounce laziness and be busy as ants, and makes appropriate resolutions to enhance his virtue by various plans requiring great industry. Ironically, however, these very ants are the means by which a sufficient portion of the nest is put together again to render a man invisible—as it turns out, a man who, as Michael fears, may abuse it far more than he does. There follows the appearance of an enormous pack of wolves, representing hellish spirits (as in Chapter 16 of *Springinsfeld*). Other creatures of Satan appear in the form of huge "worms" on a topped tree where Michael attempts to escape from the wolves, and he is forced to climb one of the remaining branches.

All this occurs immediately after Michael has struck out boldly on the road to salvation. The ants, then, are ambiguous in their roles—they are not only to remind us of the divinely inspired nature of industry, but are also instrumental in a work of the devil! Furthermore, a far greater punishment than the bees and the cesspool seems to be threatened by the loathsome worms and fierce wolves. Then Michael's good intentions come to naught upon seeing the nest find its way into the hands of a new bearer. Finally—irony of ironies—Michael discovers the "worms" to be long narrow bags containing the minstrel woman's ducats, which he promptly and unscrupulously appropriates! (There is *always* a curse placed on such treasures in Grimmelshausen's writings.) One more ambiguity arises when Michael expresses the intention of using the money to find and marry the girl whom he had dishonored on the night following the village wedding in Chapter 18. At the time of writing the final words of his tale, he has not yet found her.

The door is thus opened widely for more storytelling—for perhaps another sequence of adventures with Michael as main character (which Grimmelshausen did not live to write, if he intended to do so); but even more so for further episodes in the tale of the bird's nest in the hands of a new and different bearer. As before, especially at the end of Book V of *Simplicissimus,* Grimmelshausen qualified the finality of the concluding sequence, thus leaving the life as portrayed open to ever more and varied experiences. Grimmelshausen was keenly aware that until a life ends it offers always more and different potentials, and thus more stories to tell about it.

An overview of Part Two of the *Bird's Nest* yields a totally different kind of picture from the episodic mosaic of Part One. Rather than progressing in a meandering fashion from town to town, and adventure to adventure, the tenth book of the Simplician writings resembles Books I through VIII more than it does IX in composition, for it is basically and clearly triadic. Its main body, consisting of the large midsection dealing mainly with adultery (Chapters 4 through 20), is symmetrically introduced and concluded with sections in which Satanic forms of sorcery play a large role. The nest-bearer, a well-to-do merchant, does not wander nearly as much as Michael. The main body of the story consists of two parts set at only one location each, the first telling the tale involving his own and his wife's adulterous behavior, the second the story centering on his seduction of Esther. Grimmelshausen sharply and repeatedly differentiates between the matters treated in Part One, and those dealt with in Part Two. In the beginning of the second of two prefaces of the latter, he states his intention in Part One as that of reminding his readers of God's ever-abiding presence, and in Part Two that of pointing out the dangers of associations with the evil spirit. This is supported by the verse-motto at the beginning of the text, which sternly warns of the devil, sin, and its punishment in Hell. The frontispiece illustrates the scene at the beginning of Chapter 3, in which the strange little sorcerer has conjured up the dragonlike creature with the head of a beautiful woman, as he stands with the merchant inside a magic circle. In contrast to the frontispiece of Part One, this one does not present a complex allegory, but merely an episode central to the moral content of the story. We are not led to expect a tale of the tortuous ways and the deceptive appearances of the world as experienced by Michael. Part Two is about devilishness, pure and simple, from beginning to end, along with constant warnings against it—especially when it is made to appear to be as appealing as the face of the dragon on the frontispiece.

Chapters 1 to 3 comprise the opening section. In the first chapter, the merchant condemns, in retrospect, the sins he has committed—greed, lust and sorcery. He makes reference to the point of departure of his story, i.e., the theft reported in *Springinsfeld* of a considerable sum of his money by the minstrel woman. The possibility of his avoiding all the iniquity of the episodes to follow is presented in Chapter 2, when he contemplates the emblematic meaning of the flowers that grow from bulbs in his garden. They remind him of ever-present hope for the future. This "reading" of God's Word from the "Book of Nature" leads, for the moment, to resolutions to lead a better life. But the spectral appearance of the little "wandering scholar"—obviously a devil in disguise—puts a stop to his more virtuous musings. The passage that follows in Chapter 3 offers us a masterful conjuration scene. It includes a magic wand, a magic circle, and a conjuration—first of the repulsive dragon-lady, then of the goddess Fortuna. Then there is the curious mumbo-jumbo about the merchant's stolen money being accessible only if it has not yet been seen by someone else (it has, of course, by Michael!). Of greatest interest is the alternative that the merchant has of claiming the bird's nest instead of his money. This final scene of the book's introductory chapter, then, graphically emphasizes the *satanic* origin and nature of the bird's nest, and thus to what it has in store for the merchant. That he could have chosen not to pursue this course is made clear at two junctures: first, when, after interpreting the meaning of the flower bulbs, he elects instead to follow the wandering scholar; and, secondly, when he opts for the nest rather than for his money.[54] No doubt, in view of what subsequently happens, he has chosen the greater of two evils.

The first in the series of events that follow in Chapters 4 through 10 is the discovery of his wife's intention to commit adultery. The series of bawdy bedroom conspiracies and lurid seduction scenes serves to enmesh the merchant into ever more serious offenses. It is made clear that his revenge (adultery with the maid) and his crude punishment of his wife's "wrongdoing" (she never does, after all, really carry out her intention, although she thinks that she does) are designed more to justify his own pleasurable wallowing than to serve as an instrument of God's justice, in Michael's sense. In retrospect, the merchant points out the irony of his punishing her for adultery while he is delighting in the maid's favors far more than his wife is enjoying "her lover," who is really he himself in disguise. He also realizes the peril stemming from his earlier choice to ignore God's word in his pursuit of wealth and his recourse to sorcery.[55]

This part of the story, then, with all of its rationalizations, motivates and prepares the merchant for the monstrous acts of the central set of episodes taking place in the Amsterdam ghetto. The short interlude of Chapter 10, concerning the seduced, abandoned, and pregnant young lady who is advised by her aunt to give birth in secret, and then to marry someone else, not only gives further evidence of the ubiquity of illicit lovemaking, but makes the final point that women, particularly in such matters, are not to be trusted! A ruse designed to mislead the new suitor into believing that his bride is a virgin is presented as an integral part of this sultry, bedroom world, as with the maid and manservant of the merchant. Later this ruse finds a new variation in the marriage of Esther and Erasmus.

The merchant's adventures in the Amsterdam ghetto (Chapters 11 through 20) are introduced and concluded in a significant way—with episodes involving both sorcery and war. In Chapter 11, he consults fortune-telling astrologers to discover whether there is to be war, which was threatening Holland at this time. This is interpreted as an act related to the sorcery by means of which he obtained the nest. The long discussion between seven men about the forthcoming hostilities serves to evoke the charged atmosphere of uncertainty in a prewar situation. This fear climaxes at the beginning of Chapter 12, when the possibility that a war between France and Holland could spread throughout all of Europe is considered—a horrifying prospect with the Thirty Years' War still in the memory of many. Then the outright prophecy of the song which the merchant overhears recalls the specter of war, as depicted in *Simplicissimus*, all the more vividly, and ironically concludes with the statement that "without war, pestilence, and hunger, the world could not again be improved."[56] This statement is immediately juxtaposed with the nest-bearer's entry into Eliezer's house to rob him, followed by the sight of Esther embroidering.

The description of Esther is a masterpiece of vivid portraiture. It is followed by an equally well-drawn eruption of passion in the invisible viewer, who indulges in the verbal extravagances of the Petrarchan lover. We are reminded that Satan is behind all this.[57] The sin of pursuing money is renounced but over-trumped by a greater one: the merchant's lust for Eliezer's daughter rather than for his hoard of money and jewelry. The nest-bearer then enters on a course in which his entanglement is further complicated by a variety of additional wrongdoings in a plot to seduce Esther. He first enters the sinister underworld which seventeenth-century Jewry represented to the Christian, and dabbles extensively in its folklore. (Grimmelshausen demonstrates here an enthusiasm and breadth of knowledge in things Judaic that might have made *him* suspect to his times!) In the numerically central Chapter 14, he creates a series of miracles involving his impersonation of the Archangel Uriel (chosen apparently for the play on words with "Urian," a euphemism for the devil)[58] and of the prophet Elijah, who is omnipresent in Jewish folklore. His sin here lies in the strengthening of the faith of the Jewish community in its supposedly false doctrine. His blasphemy in creating false miracles by impersonating a figure considered sacred is implicit. The first high point is his nocturnal visit to Eliezer, in disguise, by which he prepares the way for the seduction, allegedly to create a Messiah.

The extreme sensuousness of the cohabitation with Esther in Chapter 15 conforms to our expectations, but its outcome is unexpected. One of Grimmelshausen's most magnificent ironical inventions is Esther's delivery of a *girl*. This part of the story being capped with such a masterfully abrupt cut-off, he immediately begins another—that of the courtship and marriage of Esther and Erasmus. The plot that is spun here is fully worthy of this position in the tale, in which an anticlimactic effect must be avoided. But it consists of more than clever, entertaining ruses. In the course of Chapters 16 through 20, a character of impressive, even potentially tragic, dignity is created in the figure of Erasmus, the converted Jew who is not wholly acceptable to members of either his former or his new congregation. His wavering faith upon hearing of the coming of the Messiah, his hopes for the future in the East Indies, his suffering upon hearing of the merchant's, his friend's, misdeeds, his successful admonitions to him to better his ways—all these things combine to lend him an impressive wholeness of character.

This section of the story is concluded with another touch of irony, increased, as it were, to the second power. For, as Esther comes ever closer to the time of her departure as Erasmus' wife in Chapter 20, the merchant, although he has arranged the match, comes to love Esther more and more and vainly wishes that he could take Erasmus' place. It is suggested that this torment (like the bees that attack Michael in Part One) is a just punishment.[59] This, however, is nothing compared with his agony when, after the wedding, the merchant receives word that his wife has died, and thus learns that he could have married Esther after all. The ultimate manifestation of his depravity occurs when, in his insane rage brought about by Esther's inaccessibility, he is about to murder his good friend—a deed forestalled by Erasmus' suspicions and his sudden departure with his newly-acquired family. A touch of counter-irony, perhaps a consolation, is derived from his having been instrumental in securing three Jewesses for Christianity; for not only Esther is converted for the sake of her new husband, but also her servant-woman Josanna; and, of course, the merchant's daughter is baptized.

The merchant is, however, far from salvation. Chapter 21 first shows him plunging into debauchery to heal the wounds inflicted by the Esther affair, then dabbling in new kinds of black magic he learns from the bad company that he meanwhile has been keeping. The main body of the chapter consists of a vision created by magic in this company. Although presented as an illusion by a charlatan, the scenes which are thus conjured up provide an overview of the world *in toto* as it appears to the merchant immediately following the Esther episodes, and preceding the nest-bearer's brief career as a soldier. The scanning of the world from a visionary pinnacle is a favorite device of Grimmelshausen, as will be recalled from *Simplicissimus*. Concerning the relationship of Book X to the trunk novel, it is of interest to note that this vision recapitulates much of the sense conveyed by these visions. The beginning paints a Utopia, not unlike that inhabited by the subterranean folk of the Mummelsee episode. People unworthy of this happiness, however, are soon converted into ugly beasts with appearance and traits suggestive of their sins. The conference of the gods on Olympus, held to decide how to deal with mankind's numerous wrongdoings (with Jupiter playing a leading role) recalls the Jupiter section near the beginning of Book III. Like that madman, the god of this scene is kindly disposed toward mankind, but, when his anger is aroused (as in Book IV, Ch. 5), he finds it necessary to unleash Mars's fury on the world in order to lead sinners "by deprivation and misery to knowledge of themselves and of their failings."[60]

In spite of its devilish origin, the vision, as moralized on in Chapter 22, can teach either good or evil, depending on the observer. After examples of this principle have been enumerated, the merchant himself receives the focus of attention, and we find him toward the end of the chapter fascinated by, and even sadistically attracted to, a vision of the horrors of war that has much of the grim, martial atmosphere of the Tree of Society in Book I. When the long-foreseen war breaks out, and the merchant has become a soldier, the sin of his war cravings is compounded by his use of black magic. In addition to rendering himself invisible with the nest, he acquires a certain invulnerability through magic and is able, moreover, to cause the enemy's weapons to malfunction. This is the ultimate outrage against God, in the special terms of the book; thus his punishment is imminent. Corresponding to Michael's beestings and his immersion in filth are the merchant's serious leg wound and his being trampled on by horses on the battlefield. Thus the greater of the two offenders in the two books receives the more severe punishment.

The war and black-magic episodes (Chapters 21–23) being over, the tediously depicted process of his physical recovery, true penitence, and spiritual regeneration can now take place in the final four chapters. The full recognition of his sins finally comes about in Chapter 26, after considerable delay, and with some rationalization to his father confessor. The important point is made that it was definitely the bird's nest which was the main instrument of his evil, and that it was indeed a work of the devil—an admission that is here spelled out for the first time unequivocally, although we may have had a more than slight suspicion of it all along. With it his other magic paraphernalia, which he empties out of his pockets like a juvenile miscreant, are condemned. First these minor nuisances are destroyed by the priest, and subsequently the nest itself is again torn apart in an exorcistic ceremony, flung from a bridge, and sent on its way down the Rhine. There is a solemn finality about this action that suggests that Grimmelshausen did *not* intend to resurrect the bird's nest for another story.

The question of its resurrection is an important one in the context of the ten-book novel. One cannot deny some truth to Streller's contention that *The Miraculous Bird's Nest II* recapitulates much of the whole cycle.[61] As was seen above, this recapitulation took quite specific forms in the vision of Chapters 21 and 22. Such a summation would be altogether appropriate for the final segment of most works of fiction. Further support to the ten-book concept is lent by the finality of the destruction of the nest. Finally, there is the all-important matter of *symmetry*. *The Bird's Nest* completes a five-book unit of sequels corresponding to the five-book trunk novel. There does remain, however, the puzzling fact that Grimmelshausen opens a door at the end of Part One in a typical manner aimed at providing a point of departure for another tale—i.e., that of Michael, in possession of the merchant's stolen money (which must have a curse on it) in pursuit of the girl whose honor he wishes to restore. Unfortunately, Grimmelshausen died shortly after completion of Part Two.

There are, however, some conclusions one can draw about the bearing of the last two books on the whole ten-book unit. Obviously, Grimmelshausen's Simplician writings take a decidedly new turn at the beginning of Part One. In departing from the main characters of Books I through VIII, and not so much focussing on the nest-bearers' interrelationships with the world (they are, after all, invisible most of the time), Grimmelshausen deals with broader vistas of life, and greater numbers and varieties of people, than before. In other words, the two books comprise more of a panorama of seventeenth-century human types than the others. This is true in more obvious ways in Part One, where the meandering, episodic course is far more pronounced than in Part Two. And it is the nature of the world itself that is crucial here; Michael is relatively passive in his travels over the zigzag paths and illusory appearances that determine so much of the sequence of the work. In Part Two, a particular area involving *man's response to this world* is in the foreground

—namely the pitfalls of certain evils to which, then at least, he was perilously susceptible.

In evaluating the two parts, then, a fair judgment requires consideration of both internal and external matters, as weaknesses in one area may be strengths in another. This is particularly true in dealing with Part One—which, taken by itself, at first appears to be seriously incoherent. The author of one of the most astute discussions of the work could still not avoid calling it "a series of sometimes fragmentary episodes fusing into no coherent narrative,"[62] thus making Part One appear inferior to Part Two. As can be concluded from our analysis, the apparently fragmentary and incoherent nature of the work is, paradoxically, what in large measure bestows unity on the world that it depicts, for such *is* the world of Part One. From there Grimmelshausen went on, logically, to a somewhat more conventionally structured narrative sequence in Part Two. The *Bird's Nest*, then, supplements the first eight Books of the cycle in delineating their broader societal and moral dimensions. Whether they comprise Grimmelshausen's last word on the Simplician characters and their world must remain uncertain, though we doubt that their irrepressible vitality and capabilities of further development could have left him at rest for long.

CHAPTER 5

The Minor Works

S*IMPLICISSIMUS* stands unchallenged at the pinnacle of Grimmelshausen's accomplishments as a writer. Its sequels have received varying degrees of praise and censure, but still would clearly take a secure second place. All his other works have remained largely in limbo, if not unread then at least yet to be properly analyzed and evaluated as works of literature within the whole body of his writings. It would be beyond the appropriate limits of this book to present the entire complex maze of information required to accomplish this task. Therefore, the following remarks must be primarily descriptive, and the judgments somewhat tentative.

Grimmelshausen's minor works are easily divided into three categories: the lesser Simpliciana; the aristocratic prose works; and the almanacs (frequently referred to as "calendars"). The Simplician writings deal with that area of life which Grimmelshausen knew best: the world of the burgher, peasant, and soldier traditionally represented in picaresque fiction, in satire, and in the didactic tract. The aristocratic works, mainly prose fiction, are set partly in the court circles, replete with heroic scenes of adventure and war, and partly in Biblical times. They display considerable idealization of noble leaders of the time, as was customary, but seldom without some qualifications on the author's part. The aristocratic novel was, by far, the prime literary genre—at least in sheer volume of pages—used for these purposes; the tragic drama played a similar role.[1] The almanacs, on the other hand, provide a vast store of learning, commentary, Simplician information, and autobiography that have been invaluable as various kinds of background.

I *The Lesser Simpliciana*

Der satyrische Pilgram (*The Satirical Pilgrim*, Part I, 1666; Part II, 1667) is Grimmelshausen's first known published work, and shows definite signs of being an intitial attempt to find himself as a writer. Its loosely connected parts apparently provided him with an opportunity to mold, crudely at first, a great variety of materials to be used with much greater sophistication in later writings, especially in the Simpliciana. This 150-page didactic tract consists of twenty discussions (ten in each part) under such rubrics as God, man, peasants, wine, beauty, women, poetry, tobacco, war, medicine, and others in equally arbitrary order and relative importance to each other. Each of these divisions is subdivided into three parts: "Satz," "Gegensatz," "Nachklang," (thesis, antithesis, echo). Part I is relatively lifeless and derivative (mainly from Garzoni); while Part II, published one year after after Part I, bears the definite stamp of its author's style and personality. Part II was apparently written close to, or simultaneously with, *Simplicissimus,* since the novel is mentioned only in Part II. Also there are numerous passages which are closely related in content to it. In this work's social and moral criticism (indicated by the word "satirical" in the title), in its religious-didactic messages ("Pilgrim"), in its rigidly symmetrical structure, and in its folksiness, *The Satirical Pilgrim* is of interest primarily as a prelude to *Simplicissimus.* The qualitative improvement in Part II reveals the remarkable fact that Grimmelshausen developed from a beginner into a writer of the first magnitude in about a year's time, with little or no previous indications thereof.

There are eight more minor Simpliciana, greatly varying in merit and interest. *Der erste Beernhäuter (The First Sluggard,* 1670) is a mildly amusing anecdote derived from a folk etymology of a common German word for an idler (*Bärenhäuter*); it has no specific connection with the plot of the ten-book novel. *Simplicissimi wunderliche Gauckel-Tasche (Simplicissimus' Strange Bag of Tricks,* 1670) is a didactic and satirical tract consisting mainly of illustrations (by Jost Ammann) [2], showing people engaged in their daily occupations and/or in misdeeds. Reference is made to Simplicius' role as folk-doctor (Book IV, Chs. 7-8). Later the book plays a part in the portrayal of the wiser and more mature Simplicius (*Springinsfeld,* Ch. 7).[3] Astrological and other symbols drawn around some of its illustrations tantalize the reader with their cryptic suggestiveness.[4] *Die verkehrte Welt* (*The Topsy-Turvy World,* 1672) derives from Moscherosch [5] its conception of a trip through hell as the occasion for moralizing, much in the manner of Simplicius' tirade during the Mummelsee episode, where mock praise is bestowed on conditions that are the very opposite of the morally appropriate ones (Book V, Ch. 15). In quality and importance *Rathstübel Plutonis* (*Plutus' Council-Chamber*, 1672) rises far above the other minor Simpliciana, particularly in connection with *Springinsfeld*. It has already been discussed in detail in Chapter 4. *Der stoltze Melcher* (*Proud Melchior*, 1672) is a frankly propagandistic work warning young men against Louis XIV's recruiters seeking cannon fodder for France's war against Holland. Yet it is a relatively rich and subtle piece of short narrative. Its situation is well conceived: an idler, lying behind a bush by a roadside, is the unseen observer of a dramatic scene in which a young but bedraggled man returns from the war and becomes reconciled with his parents, from whom he has been estranged. Thus we have here a prefiguration of the invisible narrators of *The Miraculous Bird's Nest*. The argumentation against the war is subtly and effectively developed: Grimmelshausen even sets the scene significantly on an overgrown farm destroyed by the Thirty Years' War. The ephemeral issue of resistance to a particular unjust war is, for us, easily superseded by other factors: the dramatic sequence involving the parents' ultimate acceptance of their son, given up for lost as a wayward scoundrel; the amusing and satirical dialogue; and the microcosmic dimensions the little work takes on when all the persons who are finally gathered to settle the dispute form a panorama of the society of the time, including the nobility and the clergy. This minor masterpiece deserves more attention than it has hitherto received.

Der Bart-Krieg (*The Beard-War*, 1673), is a mock polemic conceived for the purpose of defending those wearing a red beard (which Grimmelshausen himself sported) [6] against slander. *Der Teutsche Michel* (*German Michael*, 1673) constitutes Grimmelshausen's special contribution to the incessant discussion in seventeenth-century literary circles about the German language. It is a carefully structured tract (perhaps patterned after the five-part sequence of a drama),[7] and stylistically on a very high level—especially in the more satirical sections. It, too, is a minor masterpiece. Perhaps its most impressive feature is the finely balanced attitudes toward the various factions in the movement to create a new German literary language. On the whole, the author argues convincingly (but with qualifications) on the side of most of the various participants—purism, antipurism, cultural nationalism, cultural internationalism, dialect influence, furtherance of the standard written language, each having its definite but limited role in the process. The basic problems are by no means resolved; instead, *Grimmelshausen* presents a panorama of figures influencing the vast organic entity that constitutes a language.

Das Galgen-Männlin (*The Mandrake*, 1673) consists of a lengthy letter written by Simplicius to his son, and copiously annotated by a fictitious editor. Part of the satirical message of *German Michael* is whimsically conveyed by the omission of unnecessary unaccented "e's"—one of the proposals made by the linguistic purists. A closely related set of themes makes it relevant to *Simplicissimus* and its sequels: black magic and witchcraft (especially the use of the mandrake root); the acquisition of money; and the satanic powers lurking behind both activities, against which the elder Simplicius firmly admonishes. A wealth of anecdotes and allusions to Grimmelshausen's reading and personal experience provides considerable insight and information regarding otherwise unknown areas of his life, particularly his knowledge of, and ideas concerning, witchcraft and magic.

These minor Simpliciana, including a few minor masterpieces, reveal in their totality the tremendous creative potential inherent in the Simplician world—a vast, teeming, and vital cosmos. There is something of special interest in each of them, and together they constitute in their sum total a significant supplement to the ten-book novel.

II *Aristocratic Fiction*

The four works under this heading—*Chaste Joseph, Ratio Status, Dietwalt and Amelinde,* and *Proximus and Lympida*—may, at first, appear to be anomalies, for they differ so markedly from the author's Simplician writings. It is tempting to dismiss them as feeble and abortive attempts to cultivate the refined genres of Baroque literature for which an overambitious Grimmelshausen supposedly had neither the background nor the talent. Such an attitude has at least been implicit in the fact that only *Chaste Joseph* was republished until recently, and then only once.[8] Something more than the summary dismissal that they usually receive is, we believe, appropriate.

Der keusche Joseph (*Chaste Joseph*, 1666 and 1670[2]) was Grimmelshausen's first work of fiction, and was written after *The Satirical Pilgrim* but probably before most of *Simplicissimus*. The novel retells the Biblical tale of Joseph in Egypt, following the basic plot of the Old Testament, but also relying on a few other sources (Josephus Flavius and Adam Olearius). Grimmelshausen shaped and modified the materials of the story with considerable ingenuity and narrative skill. Joseph's fortunes rise and fall rhythmically in typical seventeenth-century style. Most characters are well-drawn and interact with dramatic intensity. Joseph himself is primarily an idealized aristocratic figure, but there are pronounced touches of folksy realism in the colloquial style in which he often speaks. He is given an especially sympathetic portrayal when at one point he labors as a blacksmith. The work's brevity— 127 pages in the presently available edition—is an outward sign of its economy, simplicity and directness—rare qualities for a Baroque novel, especially one of the aristocratic variety. We must conclude, then, that this short novel is as significant and deserving to be read and discussed as many of the Simpliciana, for it constitutes an important and distinct variation among the creations of the aristocratic burgher Grimmelshausen. He could not remain long in the rarefied atmosphere of aristocratic fiction, however, for the sequel, *Joseph Musai*, depicts a *Schaffner* ("steward"), whose adventurous life-story definitely departs from the realm of *Joseph* and amounts to what might be called a Biblical picaresque novel.

Ratio Status (1670) is a religio-political tract dealing with the "Staatsräson," or justification for the existence of the state, which Grimmelshausen sees founded on the principle of self-preservation. Prototypes of absolutist princes are presented in the figures of Old Testament patriarchs, of whom David is the ideal and Saul the most reprehensible. The source of good rulership is seen as being trust in God, as exemplified by David. The text frequently offers satirical passages that bring to mind the political satire voiced in *Simplicissimus* by the main character in Book II and by Jupiter in Book III. Above all, *Ratio Status* underscores Grimmelshausen's fundamental opposition to Macchiavelli, in favor of a state founded on Christian principles.

Dietwalt and Amelinde (1670) is Grimmelshausen's first conventional work of the type known as the "heroisch-galanter Roman" ("the heroic-gallant novel"). The plot fits the stereotyped pattern that was worn threadbare by the end of the century: idealized noble persons (in this case the son and the daughter of monarchs) fall in love at the opening of the tale, only to be plunged into a long series of ordeals and separations that ultimately serve to test the constancy of their love and virtue. They are, of course, reunited at the end, and their happy union becomes permanent. The greatest weakness of the novel lies in the frequent interruption of the action by tedious genealogical and historical passages—apparently included out of a sense of obligation to the conventions of the genre. And the telling of the story itself betrays far less of Grimmelshausen's usual brilliant inventiveness in the characters and episodes. There is, however, one outstanding feature that puts the characteristic stamp of authorship on the work: as with *all* of Grimmelshausen's aristocratic heroes and heroines, much of their virtue is developed during a lengthy period spent among the humble, in this case as farmers. Closely connected with this fact is the nonaristocratic flavor and point of view from which all this is surveyed—conveyed by a folksy style and an amusingly ingenuous tone of familiarity with nobles.

Proximus and Lympida (1672) was Grimmelshausen's final attempt at mastering the style of courtly literature. There are signs of conscious striving to be less colloquial and to handle well such elements as the flowery opening sections (dedication, poems of homage, and foreword) [9] in a conventional manner. Yet *Proximus and Lympida* is far less conventional in its composition than *Dietwalt and Amelinde*. Partly because of this very atypicality, it offers a few genuine artistic strong points. It does *not* unfold a tale of lovers' ordeals and eventual permanent bliss. Instead, the beginning of the actual love story is delayed until the end, although Lympida has long and ardently, though secretly, loved Proximus. Most of the plot consists of a series of obstacles that prevent the tale of love from beginning. Interspersed are several flashbacks dealing with the parents of the lovers. Not until Chapter 7 (of 9 chapters) does Proximus begin to woo Lympida. The work could, one might say, make up the first book of a typical long-winded Baroque novel. As it stands, it is an anomaly as far as its plot is concerned, but a fairly readable one at that. The characteristic touch in these novels helps to make it so. Proximus' parents, like Dietwalt and Amerlinde, abandon court society and take up the work of commoners (as potter and housewife respectively). This time it is not a matter of economic necessity—for they have retained some of their wealth—but of ethics, for they labor in order to avoid sloth. The "noble" hero Proximus is born and reared in this humble environment. It is no accident that a person indigenous to these surroundings is the most impressive character of the novel—namely, Basilia, both Proximus' and Lympida's nurse, who combines maternal tenderness, a keen sense of responsibility toward her charges, much practical sense, and an amusing loquacity (reminiscent of Juliet's nurse). Lympida herself holds the attention by means of her persistent lovesickness, lasting throughout most of the novel. We have here a significant variation—the feminine counterpart—of the long-suffering Petrarchan lover. At times, the detailed descriptions of her inward torment are surprisingly subtle and engaging as a psychological study. In sum, various parts of the novel are of interest and significance for miscellaneous reasons, but as a whole the work can hardly be defended as a coherent narrative. In varying degrees, this can be said of all of Grimmelshausen's aristocratic fiction.

III The Almanacs

Grimmelshausen's ten years of literary productivity were accompanied by a very significant and all-pervasive activity—the writing of almanacs. In so doing, he was participating in a tradition that had flourished since printing had come into widespread use about two centuries earlier. Grimmelshausen wrote two types of almanacs: a "perpetual calendar"; and a series of annual almanacs, which may have extended from 1671 to 1675.[10] The former is by far the more important, since in its entirety it is undoubtedly Grimmelshausen's own work and is the richer in the variety and significance of its materials.

Des Abenteurlichen Simplicissimi Ewig-währender Calender (*The Adventurous Simplicissimus' Perpetual Calendar,* dated 1670 but published 1671) was probably written between 1666 and 1669.[11] Its publication was protracted over the following two years, probably because of the time-consuming and complicated task of printing that is presented. Thus its production coincided with that of *Simplicissimus* itself, its first three sequels, and a number of the minor works. As a result this almanac is extremely useful as a source of information and enlightenment in many areas. Like most almanacs of the time, it offers its readers a vast amount of information, attached, logically or illogically, to the successive days of the year. Most items pertain to the areas of astronomy, astrology, meteorology, agriculture, folk literature (amusing anecdotes, proverbs, and the like), religious materials (holy days, saints' tales, Biblical quotations and paraphrase), and folk medicine. One of the most valuable sections for the interpretation of *Simplicissimus* in recent years has been the lengthy dialogue between Simplicissimus and an astrologer. Here the depth and breadth of Grimmelshausen's knowledge of astrology are revealed, and various individual items are valuable for piecing together the planetary structure of the novel.[12] There are a number of important autobiographical references, including the only statement by Grimmelshausen from which his approximate birth year (1621) can be derived.[13] Finally, the task of tracking down his printed sources is greatly facilitated by this and the other almanacs, since a great many books he read are mentioned or otherwise made identifiable. In Grimmelshausen's career as a writer, the almanacs undoubtedly provided numerous opportunities for the initial acquisition and molding of materials for their subsequent incorporation into his works of fiction.

CHAPTER 6

Conclusion

THERE is something miraculous about Grimmelshausen's total
literary output having required a mere eleven years to write.
Apparently this is literature born of a breakthrough of creative
energy stemming from a highly effective constellation of opportunities and stimuli in the author's life around 1665. Much
power must have been derived from an obsessive preoccupation
with the immediate past—primarily the Thirty Years' War. Nearly
everything he wrote was related, in some important way, to this
trauma in his own life and in the history of a nation which, three
centuries later, still suffers from its fragmenting and demoralizing
outcome. Grimmelshausen's role was to be the voice of a Germany
crying out against, and coming to terms with, this nightmare of
the then recent past.

The immediate and enormous popularity of *Simplicissimus* and
the *Simpliciana* in seventeenth-century Germany are thus under-
standable. Likewise it is not surprising that the relatively orderly
and peaceful eighteenth century had little interest in such tales
of chaos and war. Then, in the early nineteenth century, when
foreign armies once again swept back and forth across Germany,
creating conditions and attitudes resembling those prevailing
nearly two centuries before, we find the first revival of interest in
Grimmelshausen's writings among the German Romantics. Clemens Brentano, Achim von Arnim, Joseph von Eichendorff, Adelbert von Chamisso, the Grimm brothers, and even the older Goethe
number among his admirers. In the wake of this revival, once his
authorship had been established for the majority of writing which
had appeared under pseudonyms, his works were published in
several editions during the nineteenth century. Not until the twentieth century, however, did the revival reach the stage at which
his complete works could be published in a scholarly edition.
Scholarly activity is accompanying this important event, and
popular editions have meanwhile appeared every few years.[1]

Conclusion

It is apparent what historical phenomena are involved in the waning and waxing of Grimmelshausen's literary fame since the seventeenth century. The Thirty Years' War, the Napoleonic Wars (rooted in the French Revolution), and the two World Wars were cataclysms in which many of the orders and structures of previous times were destroyed, bringing about Ages of Anxiety, but also speculations and dreams of orders and structures above and beyond those lost. Physically and intellectually, Germany provided much of the battleground. Thus Grimmelshausen's Utopian and astrological musings, the Romantics' endless yearning for absolutes in the realm of imaginative speculation, and the creation of separate and exclusive realms of art in the twentieth century are results of similar causes—that is, radical challenges to life in the face of its threatened destruction or meaninglessness.

Grimmelshausen has some special insights to offer among the writers who deal extensively with times of chaos in Western history. He obviously had an enormous capacity for absorbing experience, and for assimilating and ordering it with a vast visionary faculty. Furthermore, for years he was directly involved in the Thirty Years' War, and survived it magnificently. His capabilities were further enriched by his peculiarly ambiguous status in society, enabling him not only to associate with all social levels, but, to some extent, to identify himself with each of them. A weaker human being could have been divided to the point of schizophrenia under the burden of such overwhelming experiences and complicated relationships, coupled with the added awareness of the fragility of life. In facing up to all the dangers besetting such a person, Grimmelshausen depicts, in his masterpiece, a figure who is keenly aware of the ultimate end of all temporal things, including his own life, and experiences anxiety and dread, which are relieved only *sub specie aeternitatis* by his Christian faith. As long as he must live in the world, however, he faces it with a combination of indomitable vitality, great adaptability, and conciliatory good-humor. His self and the world in which he lives are intricately but securely linked by the various structures created in Grimmelshausen's many narrative techniques. In brief, Grimmelshausen's works tells us, as if by an outcry, that a fundamentally imperiled life can be the most viable kind, and that stating this fully and cogently is one of the writer's supreme achievements.

Notes and References

Chapter One

1. Translated from Gustav Könnecke, *Quellen und Forschungen zur Lebensgeschichte Grimmelshausens* (Weimar, 1926), I, 142. Hereafter cited as Könnecke.

2. These and the following assumptions concerning the Hanau period are derived from Könnecke, I, 157–184, who compiled the biographical data by comparing historical documents with corresponding passages in *Simplicissimus,* Books I and II (the most autobiographical parts of the novel).

3. See Günther Weydt, *Nachahmung und Schöpfung im Barock* (Berne and Munich: Francke, 1968), pp. 311–314, for a modern German translation. Cited hereafter as Weydt, *Nachahmung.* The Latin original is given in Könnecke, II, 207–210.

4. Könnecke, I, 137 f.

5. Weydt disagrees with this generally accepted statement. Cf. his *Hans Jacob Christoffel von Grimmelshausen* (Stuttgart: Metzler, 1971), p. 2. Hereafter cited as Weydt, *Grimmelshausen.* For his reasons see *Nachahmung,* p. 23–27.

6. Könnecke, I, 123 f. and 134 ff.

7. Ibid., 123 f. and 186.

8. Ibid., I, 108 f.

9. See Könnecke I, Ch. 8 and 9 for the background of this episode in Grimmelshausen's life.

10. Ibid., I, 200.

11. Cf. Weydt, *Grimmelshausen,* p. 4.

12. Könnecke, I, 223.

13. Ibid., I, 225.

14. Ibid., I, 206 ff.

15. Ibid., I, 310.

16. See Könnecke, I, 92 for an interesting discussion, but inconclusive evidence for dating the event.

17. Ibid., I, 363 and 349 ff.

18. Ibid., I, 339 f.

19. See J. H. Scholte, *Der "Simplicissimus" und sein Dichter* (Tügingen, 1950), pp. 109–128. Hereafter cited as Scholte.

20. In the "Postscript" ("Beschluss") of Book VI of *Simplicissimus,* he states that the novel had been written "partly in his youth, when he was still a musketeer."

21. Reproduced by Könnecke, II, Tafel VI and VII.

22. Ibid., I, 380 f.

23. Ibid., I, 385, esp. note 2.

24. See Könnecke, I, 385–393 for information concerning the children. For three of them, only baptismal records are extant; this fact suggests that they died young. A son, Karl Otto, died at the age of 16 in 1675.

25. Ibid., I, 42 f. and 69 ff.

26. Ibid., II, 75 f.

27. See Scholte, "Grimmelshausen und die Illustrationen seiner Werke," op. cit., pp. 221–264.

28. See Könnecke, II, Ch. 35, 36, and 37 for a detailed discussion of these complex dealings.

29. Ibid., II, 10.

30. Ibid., II, 21.

31. An aesthetically oriented study of Grimmelshausen's style, including his use of the abhorred "chancellory style" ("Kanzleistil") is needed. It should be noted, in this connection, that in *Simplicissimus* he satirizes the prevailing official epistolary style (Book III, Ch. 10).

32. Grimmelshausen assisted in writing and/or rewriting portions of *Der Teutsche Friedensraht* (Strassburg, 1670), a work dealing with governmental and agricultural problems of the postwar period. See Manfred Koschlig, "Der Mythos vom 'Bauernpoeten' Grimmelshausen," *Jahrbuch der Deutschen Schillergesellschaft,* 9 (1965), 32–105, esp. 49–56.

33. It is not clear whether there was a serious "break" in Grimmelshausen's relations with the Schauenburgs. See Weydt, *Grimmelshausen,* p. 9 f. It is difficult to imagine how at least some strain on them could have been avoided. Grimmelshausen was, after all, discharged from their employ.

34. See Könnecke, II, 329 f. and Scholte, "Der 'Simplicissimus Teutsch' als verhüllte Religionssatire," op. cit., esp. pp. 25 ff. for further information concerning this important relationship.

35. Könnecke, II, 168 ff.

36. Weydt (*Grimmelshausen,* p. 11 f.) doubts whether Grimmelshausen could have afforded to satirize Küeffer but does not explain the reason. He does make the point that satirizations of physicians were common in the literature of the time. The sum total of the evidence still points, in my view, to the commonly accepted assumption that Küeffer was the model for Canard. See also Scholte, p. 36 ff.

37. Könnecke, II, 178.

38. See Manfred Koschlig, *Grimmelshausen und seine Verleger* (Leipzig, 1939), pp. 11–45, for the intricate web of evidence. Hereafter cited as Koschlig.

39. Ibid., p. 27 f. and 67–69; see also J. H. Scholte, *Zonagri Discurs*

von Waarsagern: Ein Beitrag zu unserer Kenntnis von Grimmels-hausens Arbeitsweise. . . . (Amsterdam, 1921), p. 81.

40. The seventh would be the *Calendar of Miraculous Tales* ("*Wun-dergeschichten-Kalender*"), considered spurious by Manfred Koschlig in "Der Mythos vom 'Bauernpoeten' . . . ." Weydt, on the other hand, presents weighty evidence for Grimmelshausen's authorship thereof in the excursus "Zum Kalenderwerk Grimmelshausens und zur Frage seiner Authentizität" (*Nachahmung*, pp. 305–307). One of the six or seven books was a second edition of *Der keusche Joseph*, but even this volume contained something new: the sequel to the novel, entitled *Musai*.

41. See M. Koschlig, " 'Der Wahn betreügt' . . . ." *Neophilologus*, 50 (1966), 324–343, which seemed to settle the controversial matter of the two different versions once and for all. Koschlig's main con-clusion is that Grimmelshausen did not write the later—greatly revised —version of *Simplicissimus* (which is called the *Barock-Simplicissimus* by Scholte), but that it is the work of the Nuremberg publisher Fels-secker or of one of his employees. The dispute about this matter, ac-cording to Koschlig, was the main reason for Grimmelshausen's de-cision to publish his writings elsewhere from about 1670 on. Weydt (*Nachahmung*, p. 306) rejects the "break" hypothesis and presents evidence for Grimmelshausen's having continued to publish almanacs with Felssecker. This discrepancy in the findings of two major Grim-melshausen scholars must remain unresolved here.

42. The Latin original reads: "Obiit in Domino Honestus et magno ingenio et eruditione Johannes Christophorus von Grimmelshausen praetor huius loci et quamvis ob tumultus belli nomen militiae dederit et pueri hinc inde dispersi fuerint, tamen hic casu omnes convenerunt, et parens sacramento Eucharistiae pie munitus obiit et sepultus est cuius anima requiescat in sancta pace." See also Könnecke's commen-tary to this text (II, 201), and that of A. Bechtold in *Grimmelshausen und seine Zeit* (Heidelberg, 1914), pp. 190 ff.

43. Three sons were still living (Karl Otto having died in 1675), and were old enough for military service. The remaining six children (if all had survived up to that point) were daughters, the youngest having been born in 1669. See Könnecke, I, 395, for more information concerning Grimmelshausen's progeny.

Chapter Two

1. See Ilse-Lore Konopatzki, *Grimmelshausens Legendenvorlagen* (Berlin, 1965), pp. 29–63, concerning the hermit episode.

2. See Könnecke, I, 6–10 et passim.

3. An additional contact that is important, though it operated ex-clusively through books, is with Georg Philipp Harsdörffer (1607–

1658), who died before Grimmelshausen's career as a writer really began, but whose short narratives provided him with numerous materials for his own tales. See Weydt, *Nachahmung,* pp. 47 ff.

4. Klaus Haberkamm, ed. *Des Abenteuerlichen Simplicissimi Ewig-währender Calender* (Nuremberg: Felssecker, 1670; rpt. Constance, Rosgarten, 1967), p. 176 (3. Materia, 1. Abteilung, Nr. LXXXI).

5. See Koschlig, "Edler Herr . . .", p. 208 f. and note 3 above.

6. Twentieth-century studies, such as Erwin Rotermund's *Christian Hofmann von Hofmannswaldau* (Stuttgart: Metzler, 1963), have tended to temper the severity of such one-sided evaluations of late Baroque literature.

7. Manfred Koschlig, "Das Lob des 'Francion' bei Grimmelshausen," *Jahrbuch der Deutschen Schillergesellschaft,* 1 (1957), 36.

8. Satire had its place in the Opitzian scheme, but it evolved into a special kind that employed more wit than humor and was concentrated largely in terse epigrams. See Martin Opitz, *Buch von der Deutschen Poeterey (1624),* ed. W. Braune and revised by R. Alewyn (Tübingen, 1963), p. 20 f. The major Baroque lyricists wrote their satires almost exclusively in the form of epigrams, although Opitz, in his theory, made allowances for a kind of "satire," which he defined as a "long epigram."

9. See Richard Newald, *Die deutsche Literatur vom Späthumanismus zur Empfindsamkeit: 1570–1750,* 2nd, improved ed. (Munich, 1957), p. 296 ff. Hereafter cited as Newald.

10. Cf. Arthur Bechtold, "Zur Quellengeschichte des *Simplicissimus,*" *Euphorion,* 19 (1912), 23 ff. et passim. Hereafter cited as Bechtold.

11. Cf. Scholte, p. 125.

12. Bechtold, p. 27 f.; and Könnecke, II, p. 323 et passim. Grimmelshausen and Quirinus Moscherosch, the writer's brother, were probably also personally acquainted. See Blake Lee Spahr, *The Archives of the Pegnesischer Blumenorden* (Berkeley and Los Angeles, 1960), p. 51 and Weydt, *Nachahmung,* p. 306 f.

13. See Werner Hoffmann, "Grimmelshausens *Simplicissimus*—nicht doch ein Bildungsroman?" *Germanisch-romanische Monatshefte,* 17 (1967), 166–180. Hoffmann argues strongly on the side of its belonging definitely to this tradition. An *Entwicklungsroman* (developmental novel) depicts a character in his evolvement from childhood into maturity. A *Bildungsroman* (formative-educational novel), on the other hand, concentrates on the process of character formation under the impact of the environment and aimed at the achievement of a state of harmony with society and the world (Goethe's *Wilhelm Meister* being the modern prototype). An *Erziehungsroman* (novel of "rearing," or "bringing up" a child), finally, is centered on the

manner of the character's upbringing. Obviously these concepts can and often do overlap.

14. Könnecke, I, 148–150.

15. For information on the hermit figures, see John Fitzell, *The Hermit in German Literature* (Chapel Hill: The University of North Carolina Press, 1961), Chapter I, esp. p. 8 f.

16. The best general coverage of this subject for Grimmelshausen is still that found in Carl August von Bloedau's *Grimmelshausens "Simplicissimus" und seine Vorgänger* (Berlin: Mayer & Müller, 1908), although it should be read only in the light of Scholte's and Koschlig's later findings. See also Hubert Rausse, *Zur Geschichte des spanischen Schelmenromans in Deutschland* (Münster, 1908).

17. The most important discussions are: Bloedau, op, cit.; Bechtold, pp. 22 f., 32–35, 40–43, 60–62, 495, 517–519; Scholte, *Zonagri Discurs von Waarsagern* . . . ; and Koschlig, "Das Lob des 'Francion' . . . ."

18. Bechtold, p. 22. Part III of the version in question was added by Martin Frewdenhold, and most of the borrowings are from this part.

19. Ibid., p. 40 ff. and 506.

20. See Bloedau, op. cit., Ch. I for details of translations and their publication. See also Fritz Ernst, "Grimmelshausens *Simplicissimus* und seine spanischen Verwandten," *Merkur*, Heft 66 (1953), 753–764.

21. Bechtold, p. 23. *Der Hirnschleiffer* and the passages obviously quoted from *Contemptus vitae aulicae et laus ruris* at the end of Book V of *Simplicissimus* are known to be Grimmelshausen's sources.

22. Fully discussed by Koschlig, "Das Lob des 'Francion'. . . ."

23. Ibid. For differing views see J. Petersen, "Grimmelshausens 'Teutscher Held,'" *Euphorion*, 17, Ergänzungsheft (1924), 1–30, in which various historical and literary figures, in combination are regarded as sources. See also G. Weydt, *"Don Quijote Teutsch,"* *Euphorion*, 50 (1957), 250–270, where *indirect* influence of Cervantes' *Don Quijote* is a prime assumption.

24. Cf. Bloedau, op. cit. Bloedau finds Balthasar Kindermann's *Die unglückselige Nisette* (1660) to be the most important novel of this genre for Grimmelshausen.

25. *Das Ständebuch: 114 Holzschnitte von Jost Ammann mit Reimen von Hans Sachs* (Leipzig: Insel-Verlag, 1960).

26. Scholte, *Zonagri Discurs von Waarsagern.* . . .

27. Ammann's probable influence on Grimmelshausen's drawings has not yet been analyzed by any scholar fully qualified to do so.

28. Cf. Koschlig (the first to have recognized this work to be second in importance only to Garzoni's *Piazza Universale* among Grimmelshausen's nonliterary sources), "Der Mythos. . . ."

29. Karl Kissel, *Grimmelshausens Lektüre* (diss. Giessen, 1928).

30. See Konopatzki, op. cit.
31. Scholte, *Zonagri Discurs* . . . , p. 95 ff. and Koschlig, "Der Mythos . . .", 63 ff.
32. Koschlig, op. cit., p. 47 f.

Chapter Three

1. See Note 1 to Chapter Two.
2. See Johannes Alt, *Grimmelshausen und der "Simplicissimus"* (Munich, 1936), p. 103; and Könnecke, I, 164 ff.
3. See Könnecke (the chapters concerning these episodes).
4. See Scholte, pp. 12–14, for a concise structural analysis on the basis of the analogy with the five-act drama.
5. See Alt, op. cit., p. 105, for a diagram somewhat like the one described.
6. This principle is basic to Siegfried Streller's whole system of numerological interpretation in *Grimmelshausens Simplicianische Schriften: Allegorie, Zahl und Wirklichkeitsdarstellung* (Berlin, 1956); see esp. pp. 79 ff. Cited hereafter as Streller.
7. See Werner Hoffmann, op. cit., pp. 166–180, esp. p. 166, note 1, and 173 ff.
8. See Alt, op. cit., p. 36 f.
9. See W. Hoffmann's conclusion, op. cit.
10. For an astute study of the two "I's" (the "narrating" and the "narrated") see Lothar Schmidt, "Das Ich im *Simplicissimus*," *Wirkendes Wort*, 10 (1960), 215–220.
11. There is a gap of about a year-and-a-half in the historical chronology. The flight of the witches also provides a dramatic and ironical scene change from the Main River northeastward to the Elbe.
12. Günther Weydt, "Planetensymbolik im barocken Roman," *Doitsu Bungaku*, 36 (1966), 1–14; *Nachahmung* pp. 243–301; and *Grimmelshausen*, pp. 60–71. See also Helmut Rehder, "Planetenkinder: Some Problems of Character Portrayal in Literature," *The Graduate Journal*, 8 (1968), 69–97.
13. See Wilhelm Knappich, *Geschichte der Astrologie* (Frankfurt am Main: Klostermann, 1967), pp. 69–97.
14. See Haberkamm, op. cit., the odd-numbered pages from 5 to 207 ("die vierdte Materia" and "fünffte Materia").
15. See note 12.
16. See Weydt, *Nachahmung*, p. 449.
17. See Nicholas de Vore, *Encyclopedia of Astrology* (New York: Philosophical Library, 1947), pp. 278–279.
18. See Weydt, *Nachahmung*, p. 275 f. For an excellent scholarly discussion of the use of astrology in literature, especially in the Elizabethan period, see Johnstone Parr, *Tamburlaine's Malady and other*

Essays on Astrology in Elizabethan Drama (University of Alabama Press, 1953). A highly important statement for the subject of astrology in literature is found on p. x: "In many instances we can construct a full explanation of what was in the mind of the playwright and the audience when an astrological allusion sufficed to delineate a large and complex system of procedures and activities."

19. Weydt (see note 11) gives the following order: Saturn, Mars, Sun, Jupiter, Venus, Mercury, Moon. This removes Jupiter two steps from its position in the Chaldean order, rather than simply reversing Mars and Jupiter, as in my analysis. The difference stems from the fact that Weydt coordinates all possible details for each chapter and section to arrive at planetary predominances, whereas I see the most important planetary symbolism in the primary roles played by Simplicius. Two arguments support my sequence: (1) it is closer to the Chaldean order; and (2) it focuses on the *hero*. This latter approach is more consonant with the novel as I have analyzed it, as one in which a single character's changing roles and fortunes are traced. Rehder's sequence is identical with mine.

20. Haberkamm, op. cit., p. 83.

21. Ibid., p. 21.

22. See Harry Mielert, "Der paracelsische Anteil an der Mummelsee-Allegorie in Grimmelshausens *Simplicissimus,*" *Deutsche Vierteljahresschrift für Literatur und Geistesgeschichte,* 20 (1942), 435–451, esp. p. 438 f. and 447 f. for remarks on the combining of satire and allegory.

23. Cf. Werner Welzig, "Ordo und verkehrte Welt bei Grimmelshausen," *Zeitschrift für deutsche Philologie,* 78 (1959), 424–430, and 79 (1960), 133–141; and P.B. Wessels, "Göttliche Ordo und menschliche Inordinatio in Grimmelshausens *Simplicissimus Teutsch,*" pp. 263–275 in: *Festschrift Josef Quint,* ed. H. Moser et al. (Bonn, 1964).

24. See also the opening sentence of Chapter 6, where Simplicius suspects Jupiter of putting on an act similar to his own in Hanau.

25. "Luthrisch/ Päbstisch und Calvinisch/ diese Glauben alle drey Sind verhanden; doch ist Zweiffel/ wo das Christenthum dann sey."

26. See Scholte, "Der *Simplicissimus Teutsch* als verhüllte Religionssatire," pp. 17–47, esp. 21 ff.

27. See Bechtold, pp. 514–518; Julius Petersen, op. cit., 1–30; Manfred Koschlig, "Das Lob des 'Francion' . . ." pp. 30–72, esp. 44 ff.; and Scholte, op. cit., esp. p. 44.

28. See Mielert, op. cit. For a discussion of indirect influence (through Praetorius), see Weydt, *Nachahmung,* p. 417 and 435.

29. Every sign of the Zodiac is assigned to one of the four elements:

thus Aries is a "fire" sign; Taurus, earth; Gemini, air; Cancer, water; Leo, fire again, etc., in the same sequence through the remainder of the Zodiac.

30. The full extent of the use of irony in *Simplicissimus* appears to have escaped most critics' attention. It receives primary emphasis, however, in Clemens Heselhaus' interpretation of the novel in *Der deutsche Roman,* ed. Benno von Wiese (Düsseldorf; Bagel, 1963), I, 15–63.

31. Cf. Scholte, p. 37 f.

32. Newald, p. 373.

33. Scholte, p. 12 ff.; Alt, op. cit., p. 100 ff.; Weydt, *Nachahmung,* p. 14 ff.

34. Weydt, op. cit., p. 299.

Chapter Four

1. For the genesis of the *Continuation,* with slightly varying details, see M. Koschlig, *Grimmelshausen und seine Verleger,* p. 82 ff; J. H. Scholte, "Die Stellung der 'Continuatio' in Grimmelshausens Dichtung," *Trivium,* 7 (1949), 325–344; and H. K. Krausse, "Das sechste Buch des *Simplicissimus*—Fortsetzung oder Schluss?" *Seminar,* 4 (1968), 129–146.

2. See Scholte, p. 325 for this term ("Stammdichtung" in German).

3. My translations from A. Kelletat, ed., *Simplicianische Schriften* (Munich: Winkler, 1958), p. 377. Cited hereafter as Kelletat.

4. See Streller, "Einleitung" and p. 129, where he states flatly, ". . . the Simplician writings were conceived, from the beginning, as a unified cycle . . ."; and Scholte, *Der Simplicissimus und sein Dichter,* p. 63. Scholte inexplicably ignores Grimmelshausen's foreword to Part Two of the *Bird's Nest.* Scholte regards *Simplicissimus* as a novel, the *Continuation* as a novella, and the shorter *Continuations* and *Supplement* as light anecdotes (p. 64). Koschlig, p. 83, states positively that the *Continuation* must have been commissioned by Felssecker, thus suggesting that it had not been in Grimmelshausen's original plans; it would follow that the remaining four books could belong to the same category.

5. See Note 1.

6. Cf. Krausse, op. cit., p. 133 f.

7. See Scholte, "Des Zonagri Discurs . . .", p. 136 ff.

8. Cf. Streller, p. 40.

9. Ibid., p. 40.

10. See Scholte, op. cit., p. 326 f.; and Streller, p. 40.

11. Chapter 5 contains the transition from the Hell allegory to the story of Julus and Avarus; in Chapter 14 the already mentioned apex

Notes and References

of success is coupled with a nadir of sinfulness; and Chapter 23 concludes Simplicius' narration, which is followed by the sea captain's
narration from Chapter 24 on.

12. For interesting theological and emblematic implications of this
metaphor, see D. Jöns, "Emblematisches bei Grimmelshausen," *Euphorion*, 62 (1968), 385–391.

13. For an interpretation of the "dark light" symbolism and related
matters in his lyric, see the essay "Das finstere Licht," in Scholte, esp.
pp. 101–05.

14. Grimmelshausen's ability as a lyric poet is best exemplified by
the well-known text of the song sung by Simplicius' father in Book I,
Ch. 7. It made an especially strong impression on Eichendorff, who
wrote a variation on it. A considerable number of poems and isolated
verses deserving attention occur throughout Grimmelshausen's prose.
If compiled, they would amount to an impressive and varied collection.

15. Cf. Scholte, p. 76.

16. This function of the *First, Second,* and *Third Continuation* and
the *Supplement* should be taken into account when considering the
doubts, voiced by Manfred Koschlig, concerning their authenticity.
See his article, " 'Der Wahn betreügt' . . . ," and Weydt's arguments
against their supposed spuriousness in *Nachahmung,* pp. 305–307.

17. For a comparison of Grimmelshausen's and Brecht's versions of
Courage see R. L. Hiller, "The Sutler's Cart and the Lump of Gold,"
Germanic Review, 39 (1964), 137–144.

18. *The Runagate Courage,* tr. Hiller and Osborne (University of
Nebraska Press, 1965), p. 238 f.

19. See Curt von Faber du Faur, *German Baroque Literature,* (Yale
University Press, 1958), p. 238 f.

20. See Weydt, *Nachahmung,* p. 81.

21. Streller, p. 50.

22. See, for a summary, J. W. Jacobson, "A Defense of Grimmelshausen's *Courasche,*" *German Quarterly,* 41 (1968), 42–54, esp. p.
42 f.

23. See Kelletat, p. 841 (note to p. 121).

24. Ibid., p. 618 ff. and 639 ff.

25. Jacobson, op. cit., p. 51.

26. Cf. Jacobson, op. cit., p. 151.

27. Hiller and Osborne, op. cit., p. 81.

28. Courage's failure to bear children is the main difference between her and Brecht's *Mother Courage*—a distinction that has all too
often been glossed over. Hiller (op. cit., p. 139) points out that her
barrenness is the crux of her quarrel with Simplicius, who is first de-

ceived into believing that she was the mother of his only living son to whom he could lay legal claim.

29. Kelletat, p. 141.

30. Cf. Weydt, *Grimmelshausen*, p. 76 f.

31. See Könnecke, I, Ch. 1 and 3.

32. Streller, p. 58.

33. Koschlig, *Grimmelshausen und seine Verleger*, pp. 225–27.

34. Streller, p. 55 f.

35. Kelletat, p. 190 f.: "When I consider the wretched misfortunes to which a soldier is subject, I am amazed that many a soldier's fancy for war does not fade."

36. Weydt (*Grimmelshausen*, p. 83 f.) found Grimmelshausen's source for the form of the polite dialogue in Harsdörffer's *Frauenzimmer Gesprächspiele* (*Conversational Games for Ladies*).

37. See Kelletat, p. 826.

38. A very large one-stringed instrument that is played with a bow. See *The Harvard Dictionary of Music* under *tromba marina*.

39. The chapter numbering is according to Kelletat. Grimmelshausen himself apparently intended that Part One should have no chapter divisions but should continue uninterrupted from beginning to end—possibly to accentuate the rambling effect by external means. (Part Two *did* have chapters in the original edition.) I nonetheless have chosen to refer to chapters, as provided by Kelletat and other editors, for the sake of convenience.

40. Streller (p. 62) describes it as a collection of humorous tales and anecdotes ("Schwank- und Anekdotensammlung"); Weydt, *Nachahmung*, p. 101, calls it a cycle of novellas ("Novellenzyklus").

41. Cf. Weydt, *Nachahmung*, p. 108 f.

42. Ibid.

43. See p. 29. The similarities between the frontispiece of Part One to that of *Simplicissimus* are, in themselves, adequate evidence for Grimmelshausen's authorship.

44. Kelletat, p. 306.

45. Ibid., p. 256.

46. Streller, p. 65.

47. Kelletat, p. 267 f.

48. Ibid., p. 290.

49. Ibid., p. 305 f.

50. Streller (p. 66) regards the moralizing passage as a "midpoint excursus" ("Mittelexkurs"), having a counterpart in Chapter 14 of Part Two. See also Streller, p. 72. To be recalled is that Grimmelshausen originally published Part One of *The Miraculous Bird's Nest* without chapter divisions. Thus the "center" cannot be found by means of the arithmetical midpoint of chapter numbers.

51. Kelletat, p. 335.

52. See p. 101, especially the reference to Jöns.

53. Kelletat, p. 267 f. and 320. An intriguing question is whether Grimmelshausen intended the same moral significance to be ascribed to Simplicius' lice in Book I, Ch. 28, and the Jupiter's fleas in Book III, Ch. 6.

54. That the second choice should be offered in the first place is puzzling, since the merchant presumably could not receive the money, for it has been seen by Michael, thus invalidating the option.

55. Kelletat, p. 409.

56. Ibid., p. 444.

57. Ibid., p. 449.

58. Ibid., p. 465.

59. Ibid., p. 498.

60. Ibid., p. 506.

61. Streller, p. 69 f.

62. Kenneth C. Hayens, *Grimmelshausen* (London: Oxford University Press, 1932), p. 189.

Chapter Five

1. See Newald, p. 354 ff., esp. 360 ff. (for the idealistic novel—though somewhat different terms are used), and 273 ff., esp. 286 ff. (for the tragic drama). The word "aristocratic" seems most suitable since it includes everything pertinent. Other terms frequently used are "heroic-gallant," "historical-political," "elegant," and "idealistic." These are not, of course, mutually exclusive.

2. See Scholte, pp. 234–241.

3. See p. 115.

4. For a partial interpretation, see Klaus Haberkamm, *Beiheft* to *Der Ewig-währende Calender* (op. cit.), pp. 34–46 and 51–57.

5. See p. 39 ff.

6. See Scholte, pp. 189–204.

7. Ibid., p. 35.

8. In Adelbert von Keller's edition of 1862.

9. Cf. Weydt, *Grimmelshausen*, p. 101 f.

10. The extent of Grimmelshausen's authorship of the annual almanacs is uncertain. That he wrote at least large sections of them seems well-established at this time. Cf. Weydt, *Grimmelshausen*, pp. 109–111 and 49.

11. Ibid., p. 35 f.

12. See pp. 73–82, and note 14 to Chapter Three.

13. Cf. Weydt, *Grimmelshausen*, p. 6.

Chapter Six

1. For the course of Grimmelshausen's changing fame, influence, and image throughout the centuries, see Weydt, *Grimmelshausen*, pp. 112–115.

Selected Bibliography

PRIMARY SOURCES

Editions

1. Complete Editions and Selections

Grimmelshausen. *Werke.* Ed. Hans Heinrich Borcherdt. Berlin & Leipzig: Bong, n. d. [1921–22]. 4 Vols. The most useful of the older editions, containing items now considered to be spurious (*Traumgeschicht von dir und mir* and *Beschreibung . . . der Reise . . . in die Neue Oberwelt des Monds*). Also uses the so-called *Barock-Simplicissimus*—a greatly revised edition—as the basic text of the novel, whereas more recent editors favor the first edition.

[Collected Works in Individual Volumes.] Ed. Jan Hendrik Scholte. Neudrucke deutscher Litteraturwerke des XVI. und XVII. Jahrhunderts, Nos. 246–252, 288–291, and 302–321. Halle: Niemeyer, 1923 ff. Still valuable for the extensive introductions and superb editorship of the texts. Includes: *Courasche* (Nos. 246–248), *Springinsfeld* (Nos. 249–252), *Wunderbarliches Vogelnest. 1. Teil* (Nos. 288–291), *Simplicissimus Teutsch, Abdruck der editio princeps* (Nos. 302–309; 2nd ed. 1949), *Continuatio des abentheurlichen Simplicissimi oder Schluss desselben* (Nos. 310–314), and *Simpliciana in Auswahl. Weitere Continuationen des abentheurlichen Simplicissimi: Rathstübl Plutonis, Bart-Krieg, Teutscher Michel.*

Grimmelshausen. *Gesammelte Werke in Einzelausgaben.* Ed. Rolf Tarot, assisted by Wolfgang Bender and Franz Günter Sieveke. Tübingen: Niemeyer, 1967 ff. When complete, this will undoubtedly be the definitive edition for many years to come. As of 1973, nine of the projected fourteen volumes were available. The introductions are devoted almost exclusively to textual criticism; as such, they are exceedingly competent and valuable. Original orthography and punctuation, including the virgula, are used. Much of the editorial work is derived from Scholte's edition (see above).

2. Individual Works

Des Abenteuerlichen Simplicissimi Ewig-währender Calender. Ed. Klaus Haberkamm. 1670; rpt. Constance: Rosgarten, 1967. The only complete modern edition of this most important of Grimmelshausen's almanacs. Photographically reproduced from a copy of the original edition. A valuable *Beiheft*, containing Haberkamm's commentary, accompanies the volume.

Der abenteuerliche Simplicissimus. Ed. Alfred Kelletat. Munich: Winkler, 1956. The best modernized edition, with extensive commentary and notes. Includes the *Continuatio.*

Simplicianische Schriften. Ed. Alfred Kelletat. Munich: Winkler, 1958. Companion volume to the above. Contains all the sequels of *Simplicissimus* (following Book VI) and a number of shorter pieces. Commentary and notes as above.

Teutscher Friedens-Raht/ Oder Deutliche Vorstellung/ wie im Teutschland bey erwünschten Friedens-Zeiten eine wohlerspriszliche Regierung allenthalben wiederumb anzuordnen und einzuführen. Erstlich/Mitten in dem Lands-verderblichen grossen Krieg auffgesetzt/ von Weyland Dem Reichs-Frey-Hoch-Edel Gebohrnen/ Gestrengen Herrn Clausen/ von- und zu Schauenburg/ Nunmehro aber Auff Ansinnen guter Leuthe in Truck Gegeben/ durch Herrn Philipp Hannibalen von- und zu Schauenburg/ desz Herrn Authoris Sohn. Strassburg: Johann Wilhelm Tidemann, 1670. Grimmelshausen revised and edited this book. No modern edition is available. See M. Koschlig, "Der Mythos . . ." under "Secondary Sources" below.

Translations

1. Simplicissimus

H. J. C. von Grimmelshausen. *The Adventurous Simplicissimus. Being the description of the life of a strange vagabond named Melchior Sternfels von Fuchshaim.* Trans. A. T. S. Goodrick. Lincoln: University of Nebraska Press, 1962. Originally published in 1912, this rendition has the advantage of being the most nearly complete one available; but it suffers greatly from many antiquarian phrasings.

Hans Jacob Christoffel von Grimmelshausen. *The Adventures of a Simpleton.* (Simplicius Simplicissimus). Trans. Walter Wallich. New York: Ungar, 1963. Stylistically a brilliant performance of the translator's art, it should be consulted for translations of individual passages. But alas! many passages will not be found, since the translator has so drastically abridged the original text that it gives the impression of being a different novel. The *Continuatio* is not included.

Johann Jakob Christoffel von Grimmelshausen. *Simplicius Simplicissimus.* Trans. George Schulz-Behrend. Indianapolis, New York, Kansas City: Bobbs-Merrill, 1965. The English style is natural and lucid. There are some abridgements, but the contents of the lengthier ones are briefly summarized. Sections from the *Continuatio* are included. Valuable introduction.

Selected Bibliography

2. Other Works.

Hans Jacob Christoffel von Grimmelshausen. *Courage, The Adventuress & the False Messiah.* Trans. Hans Speier. Princeton, N.J.: Princeton University Press, 1964. An acceptable, smooth translation of *Courage* and the Amsterdam episode of *The Miraculous Bird's Nest, Part II.* The lengthy introduction is valuable mainly for the background of literary history.

Hans Jacob Christoffel von Grimmelshausen. *The Runagate Courage.* Trans. Robert L. Hiller and John C. Osborne. Lincoln: University of Nebraska Press, 1965. The most successful of all Grimmelshausen translations in English. Thoroughly annotated. Passages from the Courage episodes in *Springinsfeld* are included in the Appendix.

Johann von Grimmelshausen. *Mother Courage.* Trans. Walter Wallich. London: The Folio Society, 1965. This infelicitously labelled translation has some of the same stylistic brilliance of its translator's rendition of *Simplicissimus* (though some liberties are taken). No annotations.

SECONDARY SOURCES

ALT, JOHANNES. *Grimmelshausen und der Simplicissimus.* Munich: Beck, 1936. Important for questions regarding the genesis of *Simplicissimus* (Alt hypothesizes that Grimmelshausen began to write it at an early date, while still a soldier in Offenburg); and for its structure (the pyramidal diagram).

BECHTOLD, ARTHUR. "Zur Quellengeschichte des *Simplicissimus.*" *Euphorion,* 19 (1912), 19–67 and 493–546. Still useful for many sources.

BLOEDAU, CARL AUGUST VON. *Grimmelshausens "Simplicissimus" und seine Vorgänger.* Berlin: Mayer & Müller, 1908. Still the most informative book on such topics as Grimmelshausen's predecessors among the authors of picaresque novels.

BÜCHLER, HANSJÖRG. *Studien zu Grimmelshausens "Landstörtzerin Courasche". (Vorlagen/ Struktur und Sprache/ Moral).* Berne and Frankfurt/M.: Lang & Cie, 1971.

DE VORE, NICHOLAS. *Encyclopedia of Astrology.* New York: Philosophical Library, 1947. A standard work in English.

ERNST, FRITZ. "Grimmelshausens Simplicissimus und seine spanischen Verwandten." *Merkur,* Heft 66 (1953), 753–764.

FELDGES, MATHIAS. *Grimmelshausens "Landstörtzerin Courasche." Eine Interpretation nach der Methode des vierfachen Schriftsinnes.* Berne: Francke, 1969.

FITZELL, JOHN. *The Hermit in German Literature.* Chapel Hill: University of North Carolina Press, 1961. Includes a section on the hermit episodes in *Simplicissimus*.

GRAUEL, RICHARD, ed. *Das Ständebuch: 114 Holzschnitte von Jost Ammann mit Reimen von Hans Sachs*. Leipzig: Insel, 1960. These woodcuts were used and imitated by Grimmelshausen.

HAYENS, KENNETH C. *Grimmelshausen*. London: Oxford University Press, 1932. Outdated, but still worthy of being consulted for its astute interpretations along historical lines.

HESELHAUS, CLEMENS. "Grimmelshausen: *Der abenteuerliche Simplicissimus*." In: *Der deutsche Roman vom Barock bis zur Gegenwart*, ed. Benno von Wiese. Düsseldorf: Bagel, 1963. I, 15–63.

HILLER, ROBERT L. "The Sutler's Cart and the Lump of Gold." *Germanic Review*, 39 (1964), 137–144. A comparison of Grimmelshausen's *Landstörzerin Courasche* and Brecht's *Mutter Courage*. Both, Hiller contends, are typical and successful products of two widely differing authors and world-views.

HOFFMANN, WERNER. "Grimmelshausens *Simplicissimus*—nicht doch ein Bildungsroman?" *Germanisch-romanische Monatshefte*, 17 (1967), 166–180.

JACOBSON, JOHN W. "A Defense of Grimmelshausen's Courasche." *German Quarterly*, 41 (1968), 42–54. The only interpretation that fairly assesses Courasche's positive features and points out the extenuating circumstances that lead her into a way of life that is moralistically condemned by most critics without consideration of other criteria.

JÖNS, DIETRICH. "Emblematisches bei Grimmelshausen." *Euphorion*, 62 (1968), 385–391.

KISSEL, KARL. *Grimmelshausens Lektüre*. Diss. Giessen, 1928. A valuable source of information.

KNAPPICH, WILHELM. *Geschichte der Astrologie*. Frankfurt am Main: Klostermann, 1967. The standard scholarly work in German.

KÖNNECKE, GUSTAV. *Quellen und Forschungen zur Lebensgeschichte Grimmelshausens*. Weimar: Gesellschaft der Bibliophilen, 1928. 2 vols. An indispensable source book for Grimmelshausen's life. Contains a vast quantity of documentary materials from archives, seventeenth-century historical and other works, and Grimmelshausen's own writings. Extremely thorough analyses and interpretations.

KONOPATZKI, ILSE-LORE. *Grimmelshausens Legendenvorlagen*. Berlin: Erich Schmidt, 1965. (Philologische Studien und Quellen, Heft 28.) A study of sources found in the many saints' legends available to Grimmelshausen.

KOSCHLIG, MANFRED. *Grimmelshausen und seine Verleger*. Leipzig: Akademische Verlagsgesellschaft m. b. H., 1939; rpt. New York and London: Johnson Reprint, 1967. (Palaestra 218.) Still the most indispensable source of information and conclusions concerning the extremely difficult problems of dating, authenticity, and other matters relating to editions appearing in Grimmelshausen's lifetime. Outdated, in part, by some of Koschlig's subsequent research. Some findings disputed by Scholte, and, more recently, by Weydt.

————. "Das Lob des 'Francion' bei Grimmelshausen." *Jahrbuch der Deutschen Schillergesellschaft*, 1 (1957), 30–73. Deals with a French source of *Simplicissimus*. Valuable for the difficult topic of the extent and manner of influence of the picaresque novel on Grimmelshausen.

————. "Der Mythos vom 'Bauernpoeten' Grimmelshausen." *Jahrbuch der Deutschen Schillergesellschaft*, 9 (1965), 49–65.

————. " 'Der Wahn betreügt.' Zur Entstehung des Barock-*Simplicissimus*." *Neophilologus*, 50 (1966), 324–343. Advances the controversial thesis that the greatly revised version of *Simplicissimus* published by Felssecker in 1671 was not written by Grimmelshausen.

KRAUSSE, HELMUT K. "Das sechste Buch des *Simplicissimus*—Fortsetzung oder Schluss?" *Seminar*, 4 (1968), 129–146. Finds that Book VI is both a continuation and conclusion but with some emphasis on the latter; hence suggests that Book VI had been planned from the beginning and forms an integral part of the novel.

MIELERT, HARRY. "Der paracelsische Anteil an der Mummelsee-Allegorie in Grimmelshausens *Simplicissimus*." *Deutsche Vierteljahresschrift für Literatur und Geistesgeschichte*, 20 (1942), 435–451.

NEWALD, RICHARD. *Die deutsche Literatur vom Späthumanismus zur Empfindsamkeit: 1570–1750*. 2nd ed. Munich: Beck, 1957. (Geschichte der deutschen Literatur von den Anfängen bis zur Gegenwart, Vol. 5.) A standard literary history of the period.

OPITZ, MARTIN. *Buch von der deutschen Poeterey (1624)*. Ed. W. Braune and revised by R. Alewyn. Tübingen: Niemeyer, 1963.

PARR, JOHNSTONE. *Tamburlaine's Malady and Other Essays on Astrology in Elizabethan Drama*. University of Alabama Press, 1953. Of great general interest for the subject of astrology in literature.

PETERSEN, JULIUS. "Grimmelshausens 'Teutscher Held'." *Euphorion*, 17, Ergänzungsheft (1924), 1–30. Jupiter in Book III of *Simplicissimus* is viewed as a combination of several historical and literary figures.

RAUSSE, HUBERT. *Zur Geschichte des spanischen Schelmenromans in Deutschland*. Münster: Schöningh, 1908. Outdated, but informative if read in the light of Scholte's and Koschlig's later findings concerning the picaresque novel and its impact on Grimmelshausen.

REHDER, HELMUT. "Planetenkinder: Some Problems of Character Portrayal in Literature." *The Graduate Journal,* 8 (1968), 69–97. Places *Simplicissimus* in the context of a number of literary works that can be illumined by a knowledge of astrological symbolism.

SCHMIDT, LOTHAR. "Das Ich im *Simplicissimus.*" *Wirkendes Wort,* 10 (1960), 215–220.

SCHOLTE, JAN HENDRIK. *Der "Simplicissimus" und sein Dichter. Gesammelte Aufsätze.* Tübingen: Niemeyer, 1950. Contains studies—mostly biography-oriented—previously published in journals, but updated and revised. A valuable supplement to Könnecke. The sole source of extensive information on Grimmelshausen's illustrations to his own works, and a few other, lesser matters.

———, "Die Stellung der *Continuatio* in Grimmelshausens Dichtung." *Trivium,* 7 (1949), 325–344.

———. *Zonagri Discurs von Waarsagern. Ein Beitrag zu unserer Kenntnis von Grimmelshausens Arbeitsweise in seinem Ewig-währenden Calender mit besonderer Berücksichtigung des Eingangs des "Abentheuerlichen Simplicissimus."* Amsterdam: J. Müller, 1921.

SPAHR, BLAKE LEE. *The Archives of the Pegnesischer Blumenorden.* Berkeley and Los Angeles: University of California Press, 1960. Contains (p. 51) an important letter by Quirinus Moscherosch that disproves Koschlig's thesis of a total break in the relations between Grimmelshausen and his publisher, Felssecker, during the early 1670's.

STRELLER, SIEGFRIED. *Grimmelshausens Simplicianische Schriften: Allegorie, Zahl und Wirklichkeitsdarstellung.* Berlin: Rütten & Loening, 1957. Extremely valuable analysis of the numerological symbols and structure of the whole ten-book Simplician novel, but suffers from oversystemization and overstatement of the valid thesis that Grimmelshausen used such devices extensively. The fullest expression of the hypothesis that from its genesis Grimmelshausen had the whole novel, including its sequels, in mind.

WELZIG, WERNER. "Ordo und verkehrte Welt bei Grimmelshausen." *Zeitschrift für deutsche Philologie,* 78 (1959), 424–430, and 79 (1960), 133–141.

WESSELS, P. B. "Göttliche Ordo und menschliche Inordinatio in Grimmelshausens *Simplicissimus Teutsch.*" In: *Festschrift Josef Quint,* ed. Hugo Moser, Rudolf Schützeichel, and Karl Stackmann. Bonn: Semmel, 1964.

WEYDT, GÜNTHER. "*Don Quijote* Teutsch." *Euphorion,* 50 (1957), 250–270. Cervantes' influence on Grimmelshausen is viewed as being *indirect.*

Selected Bibliography

———. *Hans Jacob Christoffel von Grimmelshausen.* Stuttgart: Metzler, 1971. (Sammlung Metzler, M 99.)

———. *Nachahmung und Schöpfung im Barock. Studien um Grimmelshausen.* Berne & Munich: Francke, 1968. A collection of several scholarly essays, concerned primarily with the sources of *Simplicissimus.* The most informative book on astrological symbolism and structure in Grimmelshausen's works. Contains an extensive and valuable appendix of excursuses; a complete bibliography of Grimmelshausen's known sources, and selections from them; biographical documents; illustrations; and tables.

———. "Planetensymbolik im barocken Roman." *Doitsu Bungaku,* 36 (1966), 1–14. The first astrological analysis of *Simplicissimus.*

———. *Der Simplicissimusdichter und sein Werk.* Darmstadt: Wissenschaftliche Buchgesellschaft, 1969. (Wege der Forschung, Vol. CLIII.) A selection from the main works of Grimmelshausen scholarship, mostly written in the twentieth century.

Index

Index